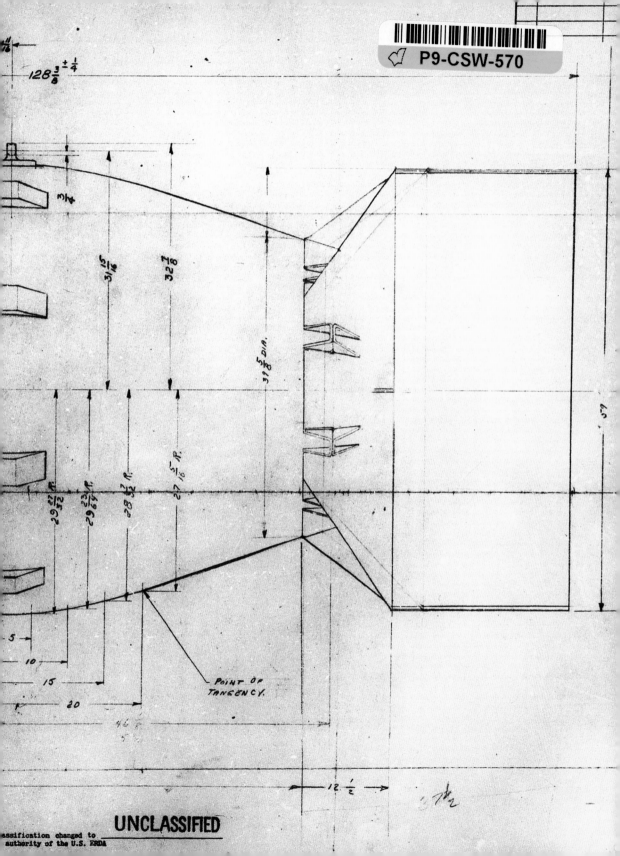

P9-CSW-570

POINT OF
TANGENCY.

UNCLASSIFIED

assification changed to _____
authority of the U.S. ERDA

THE DAY
THE WORLD
WENT
NUCLEAR

THE DAY
THE WORLD WENT
NUCLEAR

DROPPING THE ATOM BOMB
AND THE END OF WORLD WAR II
IN THE PACIFIC

BILL O'REILLY

HENRY HOLT AND COMPANY
New York

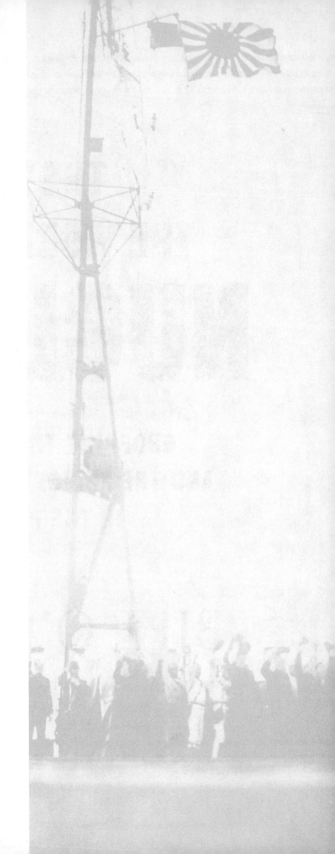

Henry Holt and Company, *Publishers since 1866*
Henry Holt® is a registered trademark of Macmillan
Publishing Group, LLC
175 Fifth Avenue, New York, New York 10010
fiercereads.com

Permission to use the following images is gratefully
acknowledged (additional credits are noted with captions):
case art © istockphotography.com; front endpaper, ii, xiii, xv,
xviii–1, 254, 255—Los Alamos National Laboratory; back
endpaper, iv–v, vi–vii, xiii, xv, 74–75, 249—National
Archives; xii—Franklin D. Roosevelt Presidential Library &
Museum; xv—Mary Evans Picture Library; xiii—US War
Department; xiv—Eisenhower Presidential Library; xii, xiv,
xv, 154–155, 243, 248—Harry S. Truman Library;
251—Wikimedia Commons.
Maps on pp. 25, 63, 95, 114, 146, and 175 by Gene Thorp.

Library of Congress Control Number 2016953764
ISBN 978-1-250-12033-5

Our books may be purchased in bulk for promotional,
educational, or business use. Please contact your local
bookseller or the Macmillan Corporate and Premium Sales
Department at (800) 221-7945 ext. 5442 or by e-mail at
MacmillanSpecialMarkets@macmillan.com.

First edition—2017
Based on the book *Killing the Rising Sun* by Bill O'Reilly and
Martin Dugard, published by Henry Holt and Company, LLC.

Printed in the United States of America

10 9 8 7 6 5 4 3 2 1

We recognize that the application of recent scientific discoveries to the methods and practice of war has placed at the disposal of mankind means of destruction hitherto unknown, against which there can be no adequate military defense, and in the employment of which no single nation can in fact have a monopoly.

—From a statement issued by U.S. president HARRY TRUMAN, Canadian prime minister MACKENZIE KING, and United Kingdom prime minister CLEMENT ATTLEE on November 15, 1945

• • •

We knew the world would not be the same. A few people laughed, a few people cried, most people were silent. I remembered the line from the Hindu scripture, the Bhagavad Gita; Vishnu is trying to persuade the prince that he should do his duty and, to impress him, takes on his multi-armed form and says, "Now I am become Death, the destroyer of worlds." I suppose we all thought that, one way or another.

—ROBERT OPPENHEIMER on the first successful test of a nuclear bomb, from the 1965 television documentary *The Decision to Drop the Bomb*

CONTENTS

A Note to Readers IX

Key Players XII

Prologue XVI

Part One: **A BOMB TO END THE WAR** XVIII

Part Two: **"DESTINATION: HIROSHIMA"** 74

Part Three: **UNCONDITIONAL SURRENDER** 154

Epilogue 237

Afterword

The Occupation of Japan:
Turning an Enemy into an Ally 241

The Decision to Develop and Use the Bomb

Letter from Albert Einstein to FDR 243

General Eisenhower's Thoughts 246

President Truman's Reflections 247

Letters and Opinions from Subsequent Presidents 249

Little Boy and Fat Man 254

Hiroshima and Nagasaki: Immediate and Lasting Effects 256

Pearl Harbor 260

Shame on American Soil: Relocation Centers 263

FDR's "Day of Infamy" Speech 265

Emperor Hirohito's Surrender Speech 268

Japanese War Crimes Trials 271

The Nuclear World 273

After the War 274

Time Line 281

The Author Recommends 285

Author's Source Notes 287

Index 295

A NOTE TO READERS

THE YOUNG ENSIGN FROM Brooklyn looks at his wife, who is holding their newborn son. The baby is big, more than ten pounds. The ensign has been back from the Pacific for more than two years and is starting a new life: as father and provider.

William James O'Reilly hopes his new son will follow in the tradition of his ancestors: hardworking Irish Catholics who value family and loyalty over money and material things. He and his bride of just over a year, Angela, are thrilled with their baby boy, whom they name Billy—William James O'Reilly Jr.

Bill and Angela married in New York City's St. Patrick's Cathedral in 1948. She already had a good job as a physical therapist at Columbia-Presbyterian Hospital in Manhattan, and it is there baby Billy is born. Ensign O'Reilly, with a college degree from St. Francis College and military training at the College of the Holy Cross, is trying to decide on a career direction. Now, with the arrival of the baby, the urgency of that decision is more pronounced.

The newlywed couple lives in a small apartment just over the George Washington Bridge in northern New Jersey. Money is tight. Already the ensign is regretting leaving the navy, where there was security and direction. Unlike many of his peers, Bill O'Reilly Sr. loved his time in the service. He learned much during the occupation of Japan, the experience bringing him a measure of respect for the Japanese people, who, in his opinion, endured the occupation with discipline.

Soon the ensign will move his wife and baby to the teeming New York City suburb of Levittown on Long Island. Here, inexpensive housing is being built, and mortgages for veterans are favorable. The price for a simple two-bedroom home is eight thousand dollars. Both Bill and Angela will live there until they die.

●　●　●

My father was always nostalgic for the navy and fascinated by World War II. He firmly believed he would have been killed if MacArthur's land invasion had come to fruition; his ship, the *Oneida*, was set to ferry hundreds of marines close to the beaches of Japan. Only later did my father find out that thousands of Japanese kamikaze pilots were waiting to attack the U.S. fleet. The carnage would have been devastating.

And so it is that Ensign O'Reilly, his wife, and their two children—my sister, Janet, arriving two years later—built yet another traditional American family over the decades of the 1950s and 1960s. My dad never prospered in the marketplace, keeping his job as a low-level financial analyst for almost thirty years. As a child of the Great Depression, he valued a steady paycheck more than anything. Thus, he settled for a pedestrian job and allowed his vast talents for communication to go undeveloped.

Not usually introspective, my father was convinced of one certainty, which he shared with me on a few occasions: his very existence, and therefore my life as well, was likely saved by a terrible bomb and a gut-wrenching presidential decision that is still being debated to this day.

But for the young ensign and his present-day son, there really is no debate, only a stark reality. Had the A-bombs not been used, you would very likely not be reading this book.

KEY PLAYERS

U.S. GOVERNMENT

Franklin D. Roosevelt: President of the United States
from March 4, 1933, until his death on April 12, 1945

Harry S. Truman: President of the United States from
April 12, 1945, to January 20, 1953

Henry L. Stimson: Secretary of war in the Roosevelt and
Truman administrations

JAPANESE GOVERNMENT AND MILITARY

Hirohito: Emperor of Japan

Tomoyuki Yamashita: Army general

Hideki Tojo: General of the army and prime minister
from October 18, 1941, to July 22, 1944

Kuniaki Koiso: Prime minister from July 22, 1944, to
April 7, 1945

Kantaro Suzuki: Admiral in the navy and prime minister
from April 7, 1945, to August 17, 1945

THE MANHATTAN PROJECT

Leslie Groves: U.S. Army general in charge of the
Manhattan Project

Robert Oppenheimer: American physicist and
laboratory director of the Manhattan Project

ALLIED FORCES IN THE PACIFIC

Douglas MacArthur: U.S. general, commander of the
Allied forces in the Southwest Pacific

Franklin D. Rooseve

Tomoyuki Yamashit

Douglas MacArthur

Harry S. Truman

Henry L. Stimson

Hirohito

Hideki Tojo

Leslie Groves

Robert Oppenheimer

Chester Nimitz

Carl Spaatz

Richard Sutherland

Chester Nimitz: U.S. admiral, commander of naval forces in the Pacific theater

Carl Spaatz: U.S. general, commander of the U.S. Strategic Air Forces in the Pacific

Richard Sutherland: U.S. general serving as MacArthur's chief of staff

Curtis LeMay: U.S. Army Air Forces general

Charles McVay III: Captain of the USS *Indianapolis*

Paul W. Tibbets: U.S. colonel, commander of the U.S. nuclear strike force and pilot of *Enola Gay*

Charles Sweeney: U.S. major, pilot of *Bockscar*

Curtis LeMay

ALLIED FORCES IN EUROPE

Dwight D. Eisenhower: U.S. general, commander of the Allied forces in Europe

George S. Patton: U.S. general on the European front

OTHER INTERNATIONAL PLAYERS

Joseph Stalin: Soviet premier

Winston Churchill: British prime minister

OTHERS

Albert Einstein: World-renowned physicist

Alexander Sachs: Wall Street economist and longtime friend of Roosevelt

Dwight D. Eisenhower

Charles McVay III

Paul W. Tibbets

Charles Sweeney

George S. Patton

Joseph Stalin

Winston Churchill

Albert Einstein

Alexander Sachs

PROLOGUE

THE AGE OF NUCLEAR MASS DESTRUCTION is about to dawn.

It has been six weeks since Nazi Germany invaded Poland, beginning what will become known as the Second World War. One month before, on August 2, 1939, theoretical physicist Albert Einstein wrote an urgent letter to President Franklin Roosevelt warning that "it may become possible to set up a nuclear chain reaction in a large mass of uranium" and that "extremely powerful bombs of a new type may thus be constructed." Einstein and other top American scientists believe that the new bombs could obliterate entire cities—and that Nazi Germany is currently racing to build such weapons.

Although Einstein and Roosevelt have met, he feels that sending the letter with one of the president's key advisers, Alexander Sachs, will be the most effective way to get his point across. Sachs finally has an appointment in October. At first, Sachs labors to find the right words to describe what could be possibly the greatest single threat to mankind. Realizing he is not being successful, he reads Einstein's letter aloud.

The president agrees to allow a group of scientists to explore the feasibility of creating nuclear chain reactions. But he doesn't see the urgency that Einstein tries to communicate.

Two years later, on December 7, 1941, Japan takes its aggression to the shores of the United States and bombs the U.S. Pacific fleet at Pearl Harbor, Hawaii. Roosevelt addresses Congress the next day. He uses the phrase that will describe the attack on Pearl Harbor for all: "a date which will live in infamy." He asks the members of Congress to immediately vote to declare war on Japan and its allies, Germany and Italy. By 1:10 P.M., the declaration has passed both the Senate and the House of Representatives.

At 4:00 P.M., Roosevelt signs the declaration of war. America has been attacked on her home soil. She is now at war. And now Congress allocates substantial funds to the secret research program known as the Manhattan Project.

The world is about to become nuclear.

Part One

A Bomb to End the War

CHAPTER 1

LOS ALAMOS, NEW MEXICO

November 1942

BRIGADIER GENERAL LESLIE GROVES and a world-renowned physicist named Robert Oppenheimer are in the high country thirty-five miles northwest of Santa Fe. They are in the market for real estate and have found a spot that interests them. It is a twenty-five-year-old boys' school with log dormitories and a stunning view of the Sangre de Cristo Mountains. It will be purchased to build Oppenheimer's new lab. In addition to the school, the government will also buy 8,900 acres of surrounding land.

The general has tasked Oppenheimer with not only building a state-of-the-art laboratory in the middle of nowhere but also convincing some of the world's sharpest minds to put their lives on hold and spend the rest of the war here.

Oppenheimer was not the obvious choice to be in charge of this

Atomic physicist J. Robert Oppenheimer was the laboratory director of the Manhattan Project, 1944. [National Archives]

The road leading to Los Alamos.
[Los Alamos National Laboratory]

top secret endeavor to build the bomb, the Manhattan Project. His past indicated some trouble: The professor from the University of California, Berkeley had a history of depression and eccentric behavior. He also admitted to having been a member of several communist groups. Also, Oppenheimer had no experience managing a large group of people. Many doubted that he had the experience required to build the world's first weapon of mass destruction.

Yet the outspoken Brigadier General Leslie Groves was

determined to hire him. "Oppenheimer knows about everything. He can talk to you about anything you bring up. Well, not exactly. . . . He doesn't know anything about sports," Groves would later tell an interviewer, referring to Oppenheimer as "a genius."

The Los Alamos Ranch School is soon ringed with security fences topped with coils of razor wire and guarded by soldiers and attack dogs. Oppenheimer's scientists come to feel so secure that

This 1946 photograph shows the center of Los Alamos as it looked during the Manhattan Project years, when about 2,700 people worked there. [Los Alamos National Laboratory]

many stop locking their front doors when they leave for work in the morning. That safety, however, comes at a cost: the personal life of each employee at Los Alamos is subject to constant monitoring by security personnel. News of the atomic bomb research must be kept from Germany and the Soviet Union.

What begins as a theoretical laboratory soon becomes a small town. A theater group is formed, with Oppenheimer himself making a cameo appearance as a corpse in the play *Arsenic and Old Lace*. A town council is elected. Parties are common and last late into the night, sometimes featuring the world's most learned minds playing piano or violin to entertain their friends.

On this high plateau, scientists work feverishly on a device designed to cause mass death and destruction. Utilizing a revolutionary new technology, the team is locking down the final design of a brand-new bomb. Shortly before World War II began, scientists discovered how to split the nucleus of an atom; the fission that occurs results in an enormous release of energy. Once news of this development leaked, weapons designers from around the world rushed to find a way to translate the research into a devastating implement of war.

The people in Los Alamos are not alone. Since September 1939, the Nazis have also tried to build what scientists are calling an "atom bomb." The Japanese, too, have been seeking such a weapon. So far, both have had no luck.

CHAPTER 2

LEYTE, VISAYAN ISLANDS PHILIPPINES

October 20, 1944 • 1:00 P.M.

ENERAL DOUGLAS MACARTHUR is grinning.

Seven hundred miles west of the island of Peleliu, where marines are now mired in their fifth bloody week of combat, the sixty-four-year-old commander of Allied forces in the Southwest Pacific leans over the rail of the USS *Nashville*. He gazes into the distance at the island of Leyte in his beloved Philippines, which was invaded by more than a hundred thousand U.S. Army troops under his command three hours ago. His counterpart in Europe, General Dwight Eisenhower, became famous for the D-Day invasion of France this past June. So MacArthur, well known for his ego, has chosen to call the date of this invasion A-Day, for Attack

After rushing ashore from their landing barges, American troops belly flop onto the sand of Leyte's beaches, October 1944.
[National Archives]

Day. The invasion of Leyte is the second-largest amphibious landing of World War II, behind that of Normandy.

As on Peleliu, intelligence reports predicting minimal enemy resistance have proven very wrong. The Japanese are putting up a fierce fight for the Philippines. Even miles out to sea, MacArthur can hear the chatter of automatic-weapons fire coming from groves of palm trees and see billowing plumes of black smoke from the jungle. Just overhead, American fighter-bombers buzz toward entrenched enemy positions, keeping a sharp eye out for Japanese fighter planes.

Two years ago, after the fall of the Philippines to the Japanese, the most humiliating defeat of his storied career, General Mac-Arthur promised the world that he would one day come back in glory to retake the islands. Now he is setting out to make good on that vow.

Douglas MacArthur, who likes to refer to himself in the third person as simply MacArthur, is a shade over six feet tall, the son of a Medal of Honor–winning general through whom he has a lifelong connection to the Philippines. Arthur MacArthur Jr. fought in the American Civil War as a teenager and, after the Spanish-American War, served as military governor of the Philippines.

"People of the Philippines, I have returned!" General Douglas MacArthur wades ashore at Red Beach on Leyte, October 1944.
[National Archives]

MacArthur clambers down a ladder hanging over the *Nashville's* side and into a waiting landing craft. As he does every day, the general wears a freshly pressed khaki uniform that bears no ribbons. He carefully maintains the creases on his shirtsleeves and trousers by changing clothes frequently, and he has just donned a fresh uniform for the landing. In case the landing goes horribly wrong and MacArthur is at risk of being taken prisoner, a loaded gun that once belonged to his father rests in his hip pocket.

Sweat stains seep into MacArthur's weathered field marshal's cap; his dark brown eyes are shielded from the ocean's glare by his Ray-Ban Aviator sunglasses, completing his trademark appearance.

Lieutenant General Richard Sutherland, his chief of staff, follows MacArthur down the ladder. After the remainder of MacArthur's group descend into the landing craft, several war correspondents join them. Douglas MacArthur knows the value of good publicity and has carefully choreographed his landing so that images of this great moment will soon be splashed across front pages around the world. The plan is to land not on the beach but at a dock. The photographers will step out of the boat first, then turn around to capture the immaculately starched and pressed general once again setting foot on Philippine soil.

Like many a scripted moment, however, the actual event will unfold in quite a different fashion.

Nine hundred and fifty-four days after fleeing the Philippines, General Douglas MacArthur orders the landing craft to sail for shore. It has taken MacArthur almost three years, but he has returned.

His landing craft arrives at Red Beach on Leyte. The general's face hardens as he steps off the boat into knee-deep ocean water, the razor-sharp creases in his pants disappearing in an instant.

"Let 'em walk," barked the navy officer in charge of directing the traffic moving on and off Red Beach when he heard that MacArthur wanted to land on a special dock. As "beachmaster," the officer has supreme authority over the landing zone; not even the great Douglas MacArthur receives special treatment.

It is forty paces from the landing craft to shore. MacArthur glares at the impertinent young officer as he wades through the water. His personal photographer, Captain Gaetano Faillace, captures the moment for posterity, even as Japanese snipers high up in the palm trees could very well be taking aim at the general standing tall in the surf.

Once on land, MacArthur is handed a microphone. His words will broadcast throughout the country.

"People of the Philippines," he proclaims, "I have returned!"

In his excitement, the normally imperturbable general's hands shake.

Soon after, General Douglas MacArthur turns around and wades back to his landing craft, which quickly returns him to the shelter and safety of the USS *Nashville*.

●　●　●

Hawaii, July 27, 1944: President Franklin D. Roosevelt discusses plans for the war in the Pacific with his two Pacific commanders, General Douglas MacArthur and Admiral Chester Nimitz, and his chief of staff, Admiral William D. Leahy (with pointer). [National Archives]

Douglas MacArthur well knows that this landing in the Philippines is a vital step toward the eventual invasion of Japan. Though plans are still in the conceptual phase, and such an assault is at least a year away, it promises to be the greatest amphibious landing in history. It is expected that hundreds of thousands of American soldiers, marines, pilots, and sailors will take part, on a scale dwarfing the D-Day landing in Normandy. The cost will be extreme—the combined loss of life is expected to approach one million people. As the most revered general in the Pacific, MacArthur will most assuredly be called upon to lead this devastating invasion.

General Douglas MacArthur's hopes for easy victories on the way to the invasion of Japan will be dashed by a determined enemy, poor strategic planning, and something new: the kamikaze—Japanese suicide pilots dropping out of the sky to sink American ships by deliberately crashing their planes into them.

CHAPTER 3

IMPERIAL PALACE TOKYO, JAPAN

November 24, 1944

BEFORE HE EATS LUNCH WITHIN his lavish Tokyo palace, Emperor Hirohito does not give thanks to a god—he *is* a god. This five-foot-five, shy, nearsighted forty-three-year-old is considered to be a descendant of the sun goddess Amaterasu, a Shinto religious deity. Today he is paying particular attention to the battle for the Philippine island of Leyte, which he has ordered his commander, General Tomoyuki Yamashita, to hold at all costs. The emperor has allowed his prime minister, the former army intelligence officer Kuniaki Koiso, to publicly compare Leyte to a momentous samurai victory of the sixteenth century.

The prime minister's public proclamations are bluster. He is aware that the Philippines may indeed fall, but he will do anything to prevent the Americans from conquering Japan. The United States would first have to take the key islands of Iwo Jima, Okinawa, and perhaps Formosa, so the Japanese have at least a year to prepare. For the past three months, a campaign has been under way to arm every citizen of Japan. Military training is now mandatory in all schools and places of employment. The nation's air defense network is being upgraded to prevent attack by American bombers, like the one that struck an airplane factory today. And Hirohito himself is involved in the development of "sure victory weapons," a form of unconventional warfare against which the Americans will be powerless.

Hirohito has approved the launching of hydrogen balloons carrying antipersonnel bombs that will waft skyward from Japan five miles up into the jet stream, which will whisk them five thousand miles across the Pacific to America. There, the explosives will detonate in cities and towns, surprising an American public that thinks it is safe from attack. In this way, the people of the United States will see for themselves that Japan will never be defeated.

These bombs will fall from the sky as if hurled down by the hand of a vengeful god. From his vast castle in the middle of Tokyo, Emperor Hirohito's divine power will shock the barbaric Americans. Of this, the emperor is certain.

The balloon bombs will indeed be launched. Most do not reach America, and those that do inflict little damage.

CHAPTER 4

YALTA, CRIMEA SOVIET UNION

February 9, 1945

THE MAN WITH SIXTY-TWO DAYS to live is being steam-rolled.

President Franklin Roosevelt sits in the pale Russian sunlight, a black cape draped around his shoulders.

Seated on FDR's left is Soviet Premier Joseph Stalin. To Roosevelt's right sits the portly, constantly chatting British prime minister, Winston Churchill.

It is morning in Crimea, and the Big Three are wrapping up their meetings at the Black Sea resort of Yalta. Clearly, it is Stalin who has emerged from this conference as the big winner.

The end of the war in Europe is now in sight. American and

The conference table at Yalta, February 4, 1945.
[National Archives]

British troops have just thwarted Nazi Germany's last great offensive at the Battle of the Bulge. Led by aggressive American General George S. Patton and his British counterpart, Field Marshal Bernard Montgomery, Allied forces are now preparing to invade the German fatherland.

In the east, Soviet troops have already captured vast swaths of former Nazi real estate, including Poland and Hungary. In this way, American, British, and Soviet troops are squeezing tight the vise that will soon crush Adolf Hitler's Third Reich. In fact, Soviet troops are now just forty miles from Berlin.

The purpose of the Yalta conference has been to define the

British Prime Minister Winston Churchill, U.S. President Franklin D. Roosevelt, and Soviet Premier Joseph Stalin pose during the Yalta conference, February 9, 1945. [National Archives]

shape of the postwar world. But even before the conference began on February 4, Joseph Stalin tilted the odds in his favor, beginning with the location. Claiming that his health did not permit travel, Stalin insisted upon meeting in this Soviet city. The truth is, Stalin feels fine—he is simply afraid to fly.

Meanwhile, a visibly declining Roosevelt traveled six thousand miles by ship and aircraft, then endured an eight-hour car ride to attend the conference. His villa room is bugged, and the servants in his quarters are Soviet spies, meaning that FDR can never completely relax because he knows his every movement is being watched.

That is as Stalin designed it.

The brutal dictator well knows that if he gets what he wants from Roosevelt and Churchill at this conference, he will rule almost half the Northern Hemisphere. Stalin's goals are straightforward: return the Soviet Union to the same size and shape as the nineteenth-century Russian empire. He now controls most of the expanse between the Baltic Sea and the Pacific, and the ambitious dictator has no intention of giving up any captured territory.

Yet there is one significant part of the former empire that Russian troops do not yet occupy: Japanese-held Manchuria, in northern China. So when Roosevelt requests that Stalin enter the war against Japan, the president plays right into the dictator's hands. Stalin agrees to fight Japan, but only after demanding that Roosevelt acquiesce to Soviet designs on Manchuria.

The Japanese and the Russians last waged war over this territory during a nineteen-month conflict beginning in 1904. Then, it was Japan that emerged triumphant, sowing the seeds for Emperor Hirohito's expansionist policies.

Soon, Stalin will have his revenge.

• • •

Franklin Roosevelt waits patiently for Yalta's ceremonial photographs to be completed. Churchill's Great Britain is the biggest loser of the conference and is emerging as a nation impoverished by war; Britain's colonies are sure to seek independence at war's end. Roosevelt is content in the knowledge that the United States will remain a superpower and that the war-ravaged countries will be divided principally between American and Soviet influences. Roosevelt has no problem with this; he likes Joseph Stalin and believes he can trust him. There is no reason the two great nations shouldn't work well together.

The stress and strain of Yalta are taking an enormous physical toll on Roosevelt. Though younger than Joseph Stalin by a little more than three years, FDR looks a decade older. The photographers capture the shadows beneath the president's eyes and the tight set of his jaw. He came into the week tired and will return to the White House exhausted. After arduous days of haggling with Stalin, the president knows that the six-thousand-mile return journey will be painful.

Inside the sixty-three-year-old Roosevelt's chest, his enlarged heart labors to beat.

CHAPTER 5

MANILA HOTEL
MANILA, PHILIPPINES

February 22, 1945

BACK IN MANILA, DOUGLAS MACARTHUR turns to leave his burned-out former apartment, escorted by soldiers from the U.S. Army's Thirty-Seventh Division. Their machine-gun barrels are still hot after the firefight that cleared the Japanese from the Manila Hotel. Beyond the hotel walls, the raging battle for this once-beautiful city has turned into urban combat, a rarity in the Pacific theater. Three U.S. Army divisions comprising thirty-five thousand men battle a combined group of seventeen thousand Japanese sailors, marines, and soldiers.

For MacArthur, who has long known the transient life of a military man, Manila is as close to a hometown as any place he has

This building in Manila, known as the Palace, served as General MacArthur's headquarters.
[Library of Congress]

ever lived. He considers the city a "citadel of democracy in the East" and has been reluctant to wage all-out war to recapture it. In fact, the general initially refused to allow the aerial bombardment and bruising artillery barrages needed to dislodge the Japanese occupiers.

MacArthur is cautiously optimistic. His material possessions are gone, but his wife, Jean, and son, Arthur, are on their way to join him, and he still commands the largest army in the Pacific. Perhaps most important, MacArthur knows his military legacy remains untarnished, despite the many months it has taken to recapture the Philippines.

A U.S. Marine approaches the edge of a shell hole on Iwo Jima to determine whether a Japanese soldier is alive or dead, February 20, 1945. He was alive and had hand grenades within reach. [National Archives]

The same cannot be said for the people of Manila. They have lost not just their homes but also in many cases their dignity.

The battle for Manila began almost three weeks ago, on February 3, 1945. On February 6, MacArthur prematurely declared to the press that the fighting was over, hailing "the fall of Manila."

That was false. Even though General Tomoyuki Yamashita had ordered Japanese forces to evacuate the city, the men left behind found their escape route blocked by American soldiers.

These Japanese holdouts have mined the streets. Concealed snipers shoot Americans on sight. The fighting takes place from house to house, room to room. No place is safe. Even after American troops burn the Japanese alive with flamethrowers and demolish the buildings in which they are hiding, the Japanese still find a way to attack; one American patrol is suddenly assaulted by a sword-wielding Japanese soldier who slices open the point man's skull before the Americans shoot him and his six companions dead.

Knowing they will never win, some Japanese soldiers get drunk and then blow themselves up with hand grenades. But many more have become obsessed with brutalizing the citizens of Manila before they die. The Japanese believe their race is superior to the Filipinos. After three years of absolute authority over the city, they are unable to bear the thought that these lesser people will triumph.

So even as they fight MacArthur's army for control of Manila, the Japanese are systematically murdering as many innocent local residents as possible.

Douglas MacArthur's rationale for not allowing aerial bombardment of Manila is that the lives of innocent civilians will be endangered, yet the horrors being inflicted upon the Filipino people defy description. Instant death from a bomb might be preferable to the agonizing murders being perpetrated by the Japanese. These war crimes are heinous even by the Imperial Army's own gruesome standards.

In the weeks to come, from February 25 to April 9, U.S. Army officials will interrogate eyewitnesses and report on these barbaric acts in detail. Witnesses will be interviewed in hospitals, refugee camps, and their own homes. Claims of injury and dismemberment will be verified with photographs taken in the presence of U.S. Army nurses and doctors. With bureaucratic efficiency and matter-of-fact detail, these reports will permanently document the barbarity of the Japanese military during the Battle of Manila.

CHAPTER 6

TOKYO, JAPAN

March 10, 1945 • 12:08 A.M.

ANNIHILATION APPROACHES AS A HARD northwesterly gale lashes Tokyo. An attacking wave of B-29 bombers flies low over the city. The *bikko*, as the Japanese have nicknamed America's most powerful aircraft, drop a small number of bombs, then make the long turn south toward the Boso Peninsula. It has been less than two hours since air-raid sirens wailed over the blacked-out city. The sound signaled the first wave of planes dropping incendiary bombs to light up the target. Tokyo has been largely untouched since the Americans began bombing Japan four months ago, so few citizens have bothered to leave their wood-and-paper homes for the safety of air-raid shelters on this clear and cold night. As the B-29s drone into the distance, the people of Tokyo feel confident enough to settle down to sleep.

Japan
1945

SOUTH
SAKHALIN

Sea of
Okhotsk

SOVIET
UNION

Miles

0   100   200   400

Manchuria
(Japan)

Vladivostok

Sapporo   HOKKAIDO
                    Kushiro
          Muroran

Aomori

KOREA
(Japan)

Sea of
Japan

Akita

Yamagata   Sendai

Nagaoka

Seoul

Toyama

Mito

Fukai   JAPAN   Tokyo   Bōsō
                                      Peninsula
Matsue   Tottori

Nagoya   Shizuoka
Hiroshima   Yokohama
Kobe   Osaka   Kawasaki
Fukuoka   Takamatsu
Sasebo   Oita   Kochi
Nagasaki

Kagoshima

HONSHU

SHIKOKU

KYUSHU

Pacific
Ocean

East
China
Sea

RYUKYU ISLANDS

Philippine
Sea

OKINAWA I.

USSR

Manchuria

Pacific
Ocean

KOREA   JAPAN   Tokyo

CHINA

Philippine
Sea

Philippines
(US)   GUAM   SAIPAN
                    TINIAN

🔥 Major cities firebombed

Map by Gene Thorp

Today, that confidence is shattered. The mournful yowl of the sirens once again floats over the city. This time, Tokyo's residents race for concrete shelters, all too aware that a second air-raid siren is confirmation that the brutal bombardment has begun. The shelters hold just five thousand people, but hundreds of thousands desperately run through the streets—fathers, wives, children, grandparents, pregnant women. Many wear packs strapped to their backs that contain their vital possessions. Worried that they may not make it to the shelters in time, fathers instruct their families to take refuge in any place that offers concealment. They throw themselves into trenches, canals, and hastily dug holes in the ground.

Inside the American aircraft, an adrenaline rush wipes out the monotony of the long flight to Tokyo; it has been seven hours since the Americans took off from bases on the islands of Saipan, Tinian, and Guam. Three hundred and twenty-five aircraft of the Twenty-First Bomber Command have flown fifteen hundred miles over open ocean to drop their payloads. To make room for an extra ton of bombs, each plane has been stripped of machine guns and ammunition, leaving these Superfortresses vulnerable to Japanese fighter aircraft. The pilots and navigators were shocked when informed of this decision during their briefing. The order is a calculated gamble on the part of the American commander, Major General Curtis LeMay. The thirty-eight-year-old career aviator is considered belligerent and brutal by some but is widely revered for his tactical brilliance.

Few Japanese pilots can be scrambled to confront the air

Bombs are loaded onto American B-29s on Saipan, the largest of the Mariana Islands, November 1944.
[Mary Evans Picture Library]

invaders, leaving the B-29s free to drop their ordnance with patient precision. Some Japanese aviators are afraid, unaware that the formidable armada has been stripped of the machine guns that might shoot them down. Harsh winds also give the American bombers an unexpected form of cover, distorting radio and radar signals. The Imperial Japanese Navy picked up the incoming flights more than a thousand miles out to sea, but due to a combination of the winds and a lack of communication between the navy and army, their warnings never made it to the Japanese night fighter squadrons stationed on the Kanto Plain outside Tokyo.

● ● ●

It is a holocaust. The B-29s drop special M-69 firebombs from the belly of each fuselage. These are quite different from the atomic fission bombs being developed in Los Alamos, New Mexico, but on this night they are far more deadly.

This firebombing of Tokyo, known as Operation Meetinghouse, is the most horrific bombing in history, worse than any other bombing of the era.

The use of mass aerial bombardment in World War II forever alters how future conflicts will be waged. The atomic device, which will use elements like uranium in order to create a single explosion of extraordinary intensity, has yet to be tested. The M-69 firebomb used on the people of Tokyo is a twenty-inch-long steel pipe packed with the jellied gasoline known as napalm. The M-69s are bundled into clusters of thirty-eight, which are then loaded inside a finned casing and dropped from the aircraft. Two thousand feet above the ground, the casing opens, releasing the bombs and allowing them to plummet to the earth separately. Three seconds after impact, a fuse ignites a white phosphorous charge, which forces the napalm to shoot out of the three-inch-wide pipe. Slow-burning and sticky, the napalm affixes itself to clothing, hair, and skin, burning straight down to the bone.

One M-69 is capable of starting a massive fire. One ton of M-69s will ensure complete destruction.

In the early hours of March 10, 1945, American B-29 bombers drop 1,665 tons of M-69 napalm bombs on Tokyo.

Driven by gale-force winds, fire envelops entire city blocks. Mobs of Japanese citizens race for their lives, only to be surrounded by the inferno and

Forty-millimeter guns fire from the deck of the aircraft carrier USS Hornet *as its planes bomb Tokyo, February 16, 1945. The men on the left are loading ammunition, and the deck is covered with expended shells.* [National Archives]

summarily asphyxiated as the flames suck all the oxygen from the air. Water mains are destroyed by the blaze, rendering fire hoses useless. Crews armed with water buckets are helpless to stop the carnage. Eighty firefighters and more than five hundred volunteers refuse to leave their posts and burn to death where they stand. Flames destroy ninety-six fire engines. Orange tongues of

U.S. Army General Joseph W. Stilwell (left) talks with Army Air Forces Major General Curtis E. LeMay at a B-29 base in China, October 11, 1944.
[Library of Congress]

fire shoot so high from the ground that they reflect off the underbellies of the silver bombers overhead.

As the heat rises, updrafts reach thousands of feet high, bringing the smell of burning human flesh to the nostrils of the American pilots. Many planes return to their home base with their fuselages coated in soot.

Soon fire consumes sixteen square miles of Tokyo. Hospitals, homes, temples, train stations, bus depots, convents, theaters, fire stations, workers' hostels, and schools are destroyed. From the safety of the Imperial Palace, which the Americans have specifically chosen not to bomb, Emperor Hirohito beholds a red glow across the horizon, turning darkest night into day.

Trapped inside walls of flame that throw off unimaginably high temperatures, citizens see their clothes spontaneously burst into flames. Debris flies through the air, striking people dead at random. City canals boil. Dead bodies bob in the rivers. Charred corpses litter the ground, many still burning.

At 3:00 A.M. the bombing stops.

As dawn rises over Tokyo, one-fourth of the city has been destroyed. One hundred thousand people are dead; forty thousand people are badly burned but alive. One million Japanese are homeless. Of the 279 B-29s that carried out the bombings, just fourteen planes were lost, mainly due to engine failures.

General LeMay's stated goal for this mission was that the bombing would shorten the war by wiping Tokyo "right off the map."

CHAPTER 7

TOKYO, JAPAN

March 18, 1945

EMPEROR HIROHITO TOURS the burned-out portions of Tokyo. His caravan of vehicles and his own maroon Rolls-Royce carry the official chrysanthemum crest, signifying that a *gyoko*—a blessed visitation—is taking place. He comes upon exhausted citizens pawing through rubble, searching for some fragment of their former lives. Upon seeing his vehicles, instead of adopting a subservient stance, the people glare. Hirohito does not engage his subjects, nor does his facial expression display sorrow or regret. Despite the war weariness so evident among Tokyo's citizens, Japan's elite will send an emissary to Hirohito two days later, imploring him not to surrender. It is their belief that the Japanese people will become used to the bombings and grow closer together in the process.

Crown Prince Hirohito arrives at the Military Officers' Training Office in Tokyo, 1925.
He became emperor the next year. [Mary Evans Picture Library]

In the weeks that follow, Japanese citizens lose sleep during more nighttime bombing attacks, leaving them exhausted and distraught. There is a rise in absenteeism in factories and a slowing of the nation's war production.

Yet the Japanese still will not surrender. Not even when General LeMay follows the firebombing in the cities of Nagoya, Osaka, and Kobe with an attack on Kawasaki.

Instead, schools in Japan close. As a sign that the nation will fight to the bitter end, all but the youngest students are put to work producing food or munitions; some are even taught how to be air-raid wardens.

But that won't be necessary. After weeks of major "burn jobs," the firebombing of Japan becomes more sporadic. There are two reasons: First, LeMay's pilots are exhausted. And second, after dropping thirteen million M-69s on Japan, the Twenty-First Bomber Command has run out of firebombs.

CHAPTER 8

ROOM H-128 CAPITOL BUILDING WASHINGTON, D.C.

April 12, 1945 • 5:00 P.M.

A LIGHT RAIN FALLS ON the nation's capital as Vice President Harry Truman strides into a high-ceilinged room, thirsty for a drink. Even after a long day presiding over the Senate, Truman appears dapper and polished.

"Harry, Steve Early wants you to call him right away," his host, House Speaker Sam Rayburn, says the instant Truman steps through the door.

Truman picks up the phone and dials National 1414, the number for the White House. Truman has not been vice president long enough to have penetrated FDR's inner circle, and calls from the

Harry S. Truman and his wife, Bess Wallace Truman (right), and daughter, Margaret Truman, arrive at the White House on the day Franklin Roosevelt is inaugurated for his fourth term, January 20, 1945.
[National Archives]

White House are rare. So even though the president is at his Warm Springs, Georgia, hideaway, recuperating from the long journey back from Yalta, Truman is quick to answer the message from the president's longtime press secretary, in case something important is required of him. So far, that has not been the case.

"This is the V.P.," Truman says at the sound of Early's voice.

Early gets to the point. "Come to the White House as quickly and quietly as you can."

"Jesus Christ and General Jackson," Truman exclaims, replacing the phone. "I'm wanted at the White House right away."

By 5:25 P.M., the vice president's car is parked beneath the north portico of the White House. Truman steps out and is escorted inside by two ushers. One takes his hat while the other guides him to a small, oak-paneled elevator. Nothing is said. Truman still has no idea why he has been summoned. Stepping out from the elevator on the second floor, he is surprised to see Eleanor Roosevelt and her daughter, Anna, wearing black dresses. Truman's relationship with the first lady has been strained, so she would never summon him for social reasons, let alone invite him up to her personal study.

Quickly, Truman realizes why he has been summoned.

"Harry," the first lady tells him, "the president is dead."

Her voice is calm, for she has known more than an hour.

"Is there anything I can do for you?" Truman asks Eleanor as the truth sinks in.

The first lady looks directly at the new president. "Is there anything we can do for you? For you are the one in trouble now."

● ● ●

The time is 7:09 P.M.

A stunned Harry S. Truman holds in his left hand a red-edged Bible and raises his right. His wife and daughter, nine cabinet members, six congressional leaders, several members of the White House staff, and a handful of reporters are crammed into the Cabinet Room. Everyone is standing. A portrait of Woodrow Wilson, one of Truman's favorite presidents, overlooks the proceedings as Chief Justice Harlan Fiske Stone of the U.S. Supreme Court recites the oath of office. "I, Harry Shipp Truman," begins Stone.

Truman has the presence of mind to correct him. "I, Harry S. Truman," he replies.

The oath continues.

Outside the Cabinet Room, a small army of reporters and photographers has gathered in the West Wing. News of Roosevelt's death has already flashed around the world, drawing a crowd of thousands to stand vigil in front of the White House.

"So help me God," Stone adds at the end of the oath of office.

"So help me God," replies President Harry S. Truman.

Harlan Stone, chief justice of the Supreme Court, administers the oath of office to Harry S. Truman on April 12, 1945.

[Harry S. Truman Library]

CHAPTER 9

OVAL OFFICE
THE WHITE HOUSE
WASHINGTON, D.C.

April 25, 1945

PRESIDENT TRUMAN IS BRIEFED on the top secret news that the United States will soon test an atomic bomb. "Within four months," begins the report brought to Truman in the Oval Office, "we shall in all probability have completed the most terrible weapon ever known in human history, one bomb of which could destroy a whole city."

If successful, this weapon could end the Pacific war, though at great loss of life to civilians. Hundreds of thousands, if not more than a million, Japanese citizens may die.

Truman knows that an alternative is the wholesale invasion of

President Truman gives his first address to Congress, April 16, 1945. [Harry S. Truman Library]

Japan. Hundreds of thousands of soldiers are expected to perish if the attack is authorized.

The invasion of Japan, however, might be unnecessary if the A-bomb is ready.

The final decision about dropping the bomb will be made solely by Truman, though at this point he is not sure what the A-bomb really is.

But Truman wants the loss of American lives to be kept to a minimum. To do that, Japan must be crushed.

CHAPTER 10

LOS ALAMOS, NEW MEXICO

April 22, 1945 • 5:00 P.M.

THE GENIUS PHYSICIST OF Los Alamos is celebrating his forty-first birthday. Sipping on a dry gin martini, Robert Oppenheimer moves from conversation to conversation in the living room of his 1,200-square-foot stone-and-wood cottage. The air smells like pipe tobacco. His guests are physicists, chemists, and Nobel Prize winners, their accents British, American, and European.

Everyone in the room has top secret security clearance, allowing each to speak freely about a topic few in the world are aware of. With Germany all but defeated, these brilliant minds are divided between those who want to see the atomic bomb dropped on Japan and those who believe it is morally wrong to destroy a country so near to surrender. Some believe that dropping the A-bomb will lead to a worldwide arms race.

It has been six years since Franklin Roosevelt's Oval Office meeting with Alexander Sachs and the resulting call to action for America to pursue nuclear weapons. Now, the "gadget," as Oppenheimer calls the A-bomb, is almost ready for testing. The detonation, when it occurs, will take place two hundred miles south, in the Jornada del Muerto Desert—the Journey of the Dead Man, as the barren, windswept landscape is appropriately known. The site has been chosen because it is remote, unpopulated, and flat.

● ● ●

Here in New Mexico, after years of top secret research, the American effort has finally moved from research to production. If all goes according to plan, B-29 bombers launching from captured Pacific islands will soon drop one of Oppenheimer's gadgets on Japan. Estimates are that the explosive force could be equal to as many as ten thousand tons of dynamite, even though the bomb will detonate almost two thousand feet above its target, never actually reaching the ground.

But those estimates are merely a guess. No one knows the exact power of this weapon.

It is not yet known which city or cities will be bombed, but a short list is being developed by the Target Committee to present to General Groves, military leader of the Manhattan Project. To measure the full power of the blast, the committee wants each bombing target to be previously unscathed. This means that the people of Kokura, Kyoto, Hiroshima, Yokohama, and Niigata, who have largely been left alone by the American bombers up until now, may soon be in grave danger.

CHAPTER 11

OKINAWA ISLAND, JAPAN

May 8, 1945 • 4:00 P.M.

SIX THOUSAND MILES AWAY from Los Alamos, the American marines know nothing about the A-bomb. "Adolf Hitler is dead. The Germans have surrendered," they are told as the battle for Okinawa enters its sixth miserable week. The news quickly passes up and down the line, from foxhole to foxhole.

To a man, the response is the same: "So what?"

These marines are trying to survive. The worldwide war that the German führer started six years ago still rages in this corner of the globe. The invasion of Okinawa brought American forces ever closer to the Japanese mainland, but there is a high price to pay for that progress—and the marines know it.

It will prove to be one of the bloodiest battles of the war.

The American island-hopping strategy began with the capture

Soldiers from the Sixth Marine Division watch the dynamite charges they planted blow up a Japanese cave shelter on Okinawa, May 1945. [National Archives]

of the island of Guadalcanal in 1942, which put Allied forces within thirty-five hundred miles of Tokyo. Capturing Peleliu in late 1944 put the Americans within two thousand miles. The surrender of Iwo Jima closed the distance to 750 miles. Okinawa is just half that to mainland Japan itself.

"We were resigned only to the fact that the Japanese would fight to total extinction on Okinawa, as they had elsewhere, and that Japan would have to be invaded with the same gruesome prospects," Marine Corps Private Eugene Sledge will later write in his book about his experiences in the Pacific.

The closer to Tokyo the Americans advance, the more brutal the fighting becomes. The invasion of Okinawa is already turning into the bloodiest and most costly battle U.S. forces will endure in either Europe or the Pacific.

Unlike the coral and jungle of Peleliu, or the remote Iwo Jima with

Allied forces establish a beachhead on Okinawa, April 13, 1945. Vehicles and supplies are offloaded onto the beach as battleships, cruisers, and destroyers wait offshore. [National Archives]

its black volcanic soil, Okinawa is a well-populated island full of farmers. Its citizenry is a mixture of Japanese and Chinese. Many have already committed suicide rather than succumb to the invaders. The verdant fields of okra and eggplant that should be carpeting the countryside have been trampled by soldiers, cratered by

shells, and littered with the detritus of war: spent casings, empty food tins, burning vehicles, and, of course, dead bodies.

The rich clay soil is now mud thanks to monsoon rains. For the first time in many months, the Japanese seem to have an endless supply of ammunition and the big guns to fire it. Poncho-wearing American fighting men cower in their flooded foxholes or attack in the slop, their minds and bodies bombarded by the sound of ceaseless shelling.

"All movements," Private Sledge will write, "were physically exhausting and utterly exasperating because of the mud" and "the ever present danger of shells even far behind the lines."

Sledge will note ruefully, "We tried to wisecrack and joke from time to time, but that always faded away as we grew more weary."

As the rain continues to pour down on Okinawa, the rest of the world waits. Pockets of war still exist in places like Borneo and China, but Okinawa is the linchpin of the final American campaign against Japan. The last great battle of World War II cannot begin until this contest is settled. In the end, five thousand of the American dead in the Battle of Okinawa are sailors killed by kamikazes. Thousands more Americans will be pulled off the line with shell shock from the prolonged Japanese artillery attacks. Japan's Okinawa casualties will number more than a hundred thousand dead soldiers.

CHAPTER 12

MOSCOW, SOVIET UNION

May 8, 1945

I N MOSCOW, SOVIET LEADER Joseph Stalin is watching the Okinawa battle carefully. He is also making plans to transport a million men across the width of the Soviet Union once the winter snows melt. Now that the war with Nazi Germany has ended, Stalin is free to attack Japanese-held Manchuria in northern China. As American General George S. Patton has warned U.S. leaders, the Soviet dictator is America's next great enemy. He is proving this by his ruthless stranglehold on the nations of Eastern Europe now occupied by Soviet forces. Stalin actually wants the war between America and Japan to drag on as long as possible, giving him more time to move his troops from Europe to Asia. It is becoming clear that as long as Soviet aggression remains unchecked, Stalin will expand his empire as he pleases.

CHAPTER 13

THE WHITE HOUSE WASHINGTON, D.C.

May 11, 1945

IN WASHINGTON, PRESIDENT TRUMAN is keeping a close eye on Stalin. Unlike FDR, Truman does not trust the Soviet leader. On May 11, Truman sharply curtails the U.S. lend-lease program with the Soviets. Their reliance on American trucks and other matériel of war, which has been in effect throughout World War II, will soon come to an end. Though the United States and the Soviet Union still consider themselves allies, Harry Truman has given the first indication that America will not tolerate Stalin's brutal global ambition.

CHAPTER 14

MANILA, PHILIPPINES

GENERAL DOUGLAS MACARTHUR does not know much about the A-bomb. In Manila, which he has not left since his wife and son arrived, the general is eagerly planning the invasion of Japan. In Washington, Admiral Ernest King, chief of staff of the U.S. Navy, and General Hap Arnold, commander of the U.S. Army Air Forces, oppose an invasion, convinced that control of the sea and skies will eventually strangle the Japanese economically, making the massive loss of American life unnecessary. It is estimated that five million American soldiers, sailors, and marines will be needed, as well as one million British troops. Casualties on both sides are projected to be astronomical.

MacArthur disagrees with the navy and air force leaders. He

believes that an island blockade will not result in unconditional surrender. He rejects the conventional notion that the Japanese are not strong enough to put up anything more than a thin defense of their homeland; they still have four million soldiers in uniform and thousands of planes hidden throughout Japan for the specific task of carrying out kamikaze bombing.

MacArthur believes his command of the largest amphibious landing in history will be successful. He sees glory. Others see death.

On May 11, 1945, two kamikaze planes hit the aircraft carrier USS Bunker Hill *in the waters off the Japanese island of Kyushu; 372 crewmen died and 264 were injured.*

[National Archives]

CHAPTER 15

IMPERIAL PALACE TOKYO, JAPAN

STILL LIVING INSIDE HIS palace in Tokyo, Emperor Hirohito ponders whether or not to move to a secret mountain fortress that has been prepared for his safety.

Japan's cities are in ruins. Hundreds of thousands are homeless. Hirohito's Imperial Navy has been almost destroyed. The nation is starving. There is growing resentment among famished civilians over the preferential treatment given to the Japanese military, particularly in terms of food distribution. Also, the emperor has known for two months that Russia wants to "secure a voice in the future of Asia"—a diplomat's wording for an impending invasion.

But surrender is still not an option for Hirohito.

Instead, he clings to the belief that his military leaders will be able to fight off an invasion of the homeland. New airplanes are

being built. Twenty-nine new army divisions are being formed. Tanks and artillery are being stockpiled for the crucial battle.

The Japanese have been preparing defenses and massing troops on Kyushu since early in 1945. An estimated 300,000 troops are gathered around the beachheads in anticipation of the American invasion. Despite heavy aerial bombardment, Japan's factories, staffed by Japanese laborers and Allied POWs, are still functioning and capable of building new weapons of war.

Japan has not capitulated to another nation in more than two thousand years.

Emperor Hirohito has the power to change all that.

He refuses.

Hirohito's nation is certainly defeated. The emperor's subjects are bleeding and destitute; their land is aflame. But Hirohito is not even contemplating surrender to the hated Americans.

However, unbeknownst to the emperor, a force more powerful than any he has ever experienced is about to be unleashed.

"If we hold out long enough in this war," Hirohito believes, "then we may be able to win."

[PRECEDING PAGES]
Hirohito, on the white horse,
returns after reviewing his
troops, 1937. The Imperial
Palace is behind the wall.
[Mary Evans Picture Library]

CHAPTER 16

OKINAWA ISLAND, JAPAN

June 23, 1945

THE BATTLE OF OKINAWA is finally won. Due to its proximity to Japan, the island now becomes the staging point for the invasion.

Fighting has raged for eighty-two days. More than twelve thousand Americans are dead or missing. Of the nearly two hundred thousand Americans who came ashore, one-third have been either killed or wounded.

CHAPTER 17

JORNADA DEL MUERTO DESERT NEW MEXICO

July 16, 1945 • 1:00 A.M.

ROBERT OPPENHEIMER PACES, a mug of coffee in one hand and a hand-rolled cigarette in the other. Sunday night has become Monday morning. His face is lined, his every movement betraying extreme tension. A hard rain hammers the tin roof above him. Outside this mess hall, lightning crackles and thirty-mile-per-hour winds lash the former cattle ranch now known simply as base camp.

In less than three hours, the A-bomb test, code named Trinity, is due to take place ten miles from where Oppenheimer now fidgets. Five armed guards stand watch at the base of the tower containing Oppenheimer's precious gadget, making sure that absolutely no one touches or meddles with the explosive. These soldiers will remain there until thirty minutes before the detonation, then get into jeeps and drive away as quickly as possible. Since a weapon like this has never been exploded before, not even a great scientific mind like Oppenheimer knows how big or far-ranging the blast will be.

But there can be no test unless this storm ends. It is anticipated that the bomb will release deadly radioactive particles into the air. Scientists have long known that these waste products of a nuclear reaction are hazardous to human life. High winds would carry them across the desert to urban areas,

Robert Oppenheimer (second from left) oversees the final assembly of the gadget inside a tent at the base of the Trinity tower.
[Los Alamos National Laboratory]

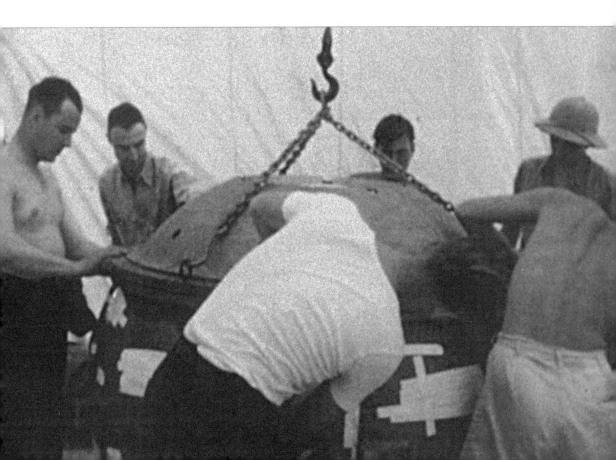

The gadget is readied for lifting to the top of the tower. [Los Alamos National Laboratory]

and rain would intensify the damage by saturating the ground with radioactive fallout. Rough weather would also prohibit observation aircraft from taking off. And on a very practical level, rain might ruin the electrical connections necessary for the bomb's detonation.

Throughout the night, Oppenheimer has tried to calm himself. He ignored suggestions that he go to his tent and sleep, instead remaining in the dining hall. At first, he attempted to sit still and read a book of poetry, but that has proven impossible. Cigarettes and black coffee are his only solace right now.

Robert Oppenheimer has the power to create a literal hell on earth. But he has no authority over the heavens. This annoys him greatly.

General Groves appears out of the gale. The Manhattan Project's chief executive is adamantly opposed to a postponement, despite the weather. The general's motives are less scientific than political: right now, halfway around the world in a small town outside Berlin known as Potsdam, President Harry Truman is attending a summit with Soviet Premier Joseph Stalin and British Prime Minister Winston Churchill. A successful, on-time detonation of the A-bomb at 4:00 A.M. will be immediately relayed to Truman, who can then share the news about the dawn of the nuclear era over lunch with his fellow world leaders. To the seventy-year-old Churchill, this will come as a triumph, for he has known about the Manhattan Project all along.

For Stalin, however, the news is meant to shock and deter. America's possession of an atomic bomb will be a vivid warning to the Soviet leader that he will be the weaker partner in any future U.S.-Soviet negotiations.

The 4:00 A.M. detonation time has been chosen because secrecy is still vital to the success of the Manhattan Project. Potential observers will be sleeping as white light turns the pitch-black desert night into sudden daytime, if only for an instant.

Groves, who is just as nervous as Oppenheimer, has managed only a few hours of fitful sleep in his own nearby tent. He is now up for the night.

The two men confer. They agree that passing the hours in the base camp dining hall is no way to prepare for the testing of a nuclear bomb. So they step into the darkness and drive four miles closer to the bomb site. At the half-buried command post known as South Shelter, a small group of technicians and scientists vital to the detonation make last-minute adjustments. There Oppenheimer and Groves reluctantly agree to postpone the Trinity explosion.

But only by an hour.

• • •

But the Trinity detonation in New Mexico has to be postponed once again. The blast is now scheduled for 5:30 A.M. With the summer storm passing, to the immense relief of Oppenheimer and Groves, it appears there will be no further delays. Groves leaves Oppenheimer at the control dugout, preferring to drive back to the relative safety of base camp. If the blast is as enormous as some fear, there is no telling whether the control dugout will be consumed or not.

At precisely 5:00 A.M., ground zero for Trinity is evacuated. The five soldiers standing guard at the base of the one-hundred-foot tower containing the bomb quickly hustle to their jeeps and race southwest toward base camp. They must drive aggressively over

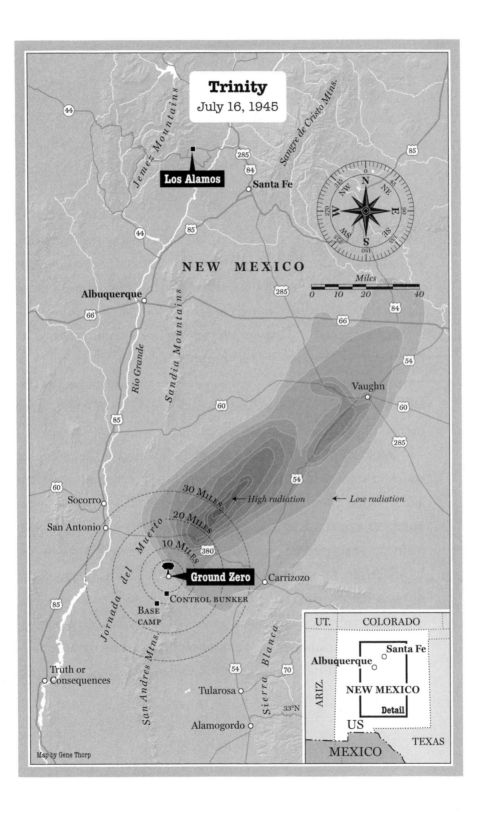

the rough desert roads if they are to arrive before the detonation. In the event of engine trouble, the guards will have a thirty-minute head start on the explosion. "I was sure that they would not walk slowly," General Groves will later write with wry understatement.

In the event that the guards are still in the open when the A-bomb goes off, they have been told to lie facedown on the ground with their feet toward the explosion. They are not to open their eyes or look at the light in any way, for it has been predicted that the flash will be so brilliant as to blind them.

By 5:05 A.M.—zero minus twenty-five minutes until the detonation—the storm's violent winds have died down to a calm breeze. A light drizzle speckles the desert sand. The cloud cover is still too thick to see many stars, which will certainly hamper the observation planes.

Oppenheimer leaves the safety of the control dugout's thick concrete walls. He steps into the fragrant predawn air and stands alone. It has been agreed that base camp is the only place where observers can stand in the open to witness the blast, but Oppenheimer plans to ignore that mandate.

There are two other bunkers just like the control dugout, each situated six miles from the blast site. Both have been covered with dirt to absorb the blast force. Teams of scientists stand ready in these bunkers to analyze the amount of energy released by the explosion and determine whether the bomb detonates in a symmetrical manner.

That is, if the A-bomb explodes at all.

A few days ago, a practice test of the electronic circuitry to spark the detonation failed miserably. Oppenheimer's engineers have promised him there will be no problem this morning. Nevertheless, Oppenheimer has made a friendly wager of ten dollars with a physical chemistry engineer, betting that Trinity will fail to detonate.

Before engineers were sure the gadget would explode, they planned to put it into this 214-ton shell to contain any plutonium fallout. When they were more confident, they left "Jumbo" hanging 800 yards from Ground Zero. It survived the atomic explosion, although its tower collapsed. [Los Alamos National Laboratory]

The desert air smells of sagebrush. Morning's first rays of sunshine are lighting the horizon. Trinity's test site here in the Jornada del Muerto is a flat patch of desert eighteen by twenty-four miles wide. Oppenheimer stares out across that broad expanse, his stomach aching from anxiety and too many cups of coffee. In the distance, he can clearly see the brightly lit tower containing his gadget. He cannot see the bomb itself, but he knows that it is a sphere ten feet across, wrapped in a tight coil of wiring. Oppenheimer himself oversaw the moment twelve hours ago when the bomb was hoisted from ground level to the top of the tower.

Inside the control dugout, Oppenheimer's scientists are behaving in an almost giddy fashion, some slathering on sunscreen in anticipation of the explosion's bright light, others laying down bets as to whether or not the bomb will light the clouds on fire.

Yet no one, not even Robert Oppenheimer, knows exactly what will happen.

An announcement over a nearby loudspeaker breaks the desert silence: "Zero minus twenty minutes."

Robert Oppenheimer gazes at his bomb and waits.

CHAPTER 18

JORNADA DEL MUERTO DESERT NEW MEXICO

July 16, 1945 • 5:25 A.M.

AT BASE CAMP, GENERAL Leslie Groves lies in one of the small trenches bulldozed into the earth for blast protection. The time is zero minus five minutes—or 5:25 A.M. All around him, scientists press their faces into the earth. Each clutches a small piece of Lincoln Super Visibility welder's glass, specially designed to protect the eyes from extremely bright light. At the sound of the blast they will be allowed to roll over, sit up, and witness the world's first atomic bomb explosion. Groves, ever nervous, finds the quiet to be intense. "I thought only of what I would do if, when the countdown got to zero, nothing happened," he later admits.

Four miles closer to the impending blast, Robert Oppenheimer feels time slow down. The sensation is torturous. So much rides on the events of these next five minutes. "Lord," he says aloud, having temporarily stepped back into the control room, "these affairs are hard on the heart."

Brigadier General Thomas F. Farrell, Groves's deputy, cannot help but notice Oppenheimer's anguish. "Dr. Oppenheimer, on whom had rested a very heavy burden, grew tenser as the last seconds ticked off. He could barely breathe. He held on to a post to steady himself. For the last few seconds he stared directly ahead."

With two minutes to go, a flare is launched to inform one and all that the explosion is near. Oppenheimer once again steps outside the control bunker and lies facedown on the ground.

At thirty seconds to detonation, the console in the control dugout lights up bright red as electrical impulses begin flooding into the bomb. There is still a small chance that the explosion might be scrubbed, but only in the event of electrical difficulties.

At ten seconds, a loud gong echoes through the control dugout as a last reminder for every man to steel himself for what is about to happen.

Chicago physicist Sam Allison, the voice of the control dugout, counts down the final seconds. "Three . . . two . . . one . . . NOW!"

A tremendous light fills the sky, a brightness so intense that those who see it will talk about it for the rest of their lives. "The light of the first flash penetrated and came up from the ground through one's lids," one observer will remember. "When one first looked up, one saw the fireball, and then almost immediately afterwards, the unearthly hovering cloud."

That cloud is purple, radiating heat that can be felt miles away. "It was like opening a hot oven with the sun coming out like a sunrise," in the words of another observer at base camp.

One hundred seconds later, an enormous boom erupts as a shock wave follows the explosion: "About like the crack of a five-inch anti-aircraft gun at a hundred yards," in the eyes of a watching ballistics expert. The explosion is so powerful that more than 180 miles away, in Silver City, New Mexico, two large plate-glass windows shatter.

At the control dugout, the blast bowls over George Kistiakowsky, the man with whom Oppenheimer made a bet that the bomb would not detonate.

"You owe me ten dollars," he screams to Oppenheimer, who is suddenly lighthearted and relaxed.

"I'll never forget his walk," one scientist will remember of Oppenheimer after the blast. "His walk was like . . . this kind of strut.

"He had done it."

Oppenheimer's euphoria and relief cannot be measured. He is cognizant of the A-bomb's wider implications. He is already haunted by what he saw today, calling it "terrifying," but at the same time recognizes the good in what he has accomplished.

As he later tells a reporter, "Lots of boys not grown up yet will owe their life to it."

Robert Oppenheimer and General Leslie Groves look at the remains of the tower. [Los Alamos National Laboratory]

CHAPTER 19

HUNTER'S POINT
SAN FRANCISCO, CALIFORNIA

July 16, 1945

A T THE SAME TIME Oppenheimer's bomb explodes in New Mexico, the men of the USS *Indianapolis* twelve hundred miles west in San Francisco are buzzing about the top secret cargo that has been lifted aboard before dawn. At 4:00 A.M., two army trucks pulled up to the dock; one contained a fifteen-foot crate and the other a small tube.

Boatswain's mate Louie DeBernardi directs the work party that now places straps around the crate so that the crane can lift it on board. Meanwhile, two sailors hoist the small cylinder onto their shoulders by running a crowbar through a small eyelet on the tube and walk the cylinder onto the *Indianapolis*.

Commander A. F. Birch numbers Little Boy as unit L-11 before it leaves the building where it was assembled.
[National Archives]

Curious crewmen gossip about what might be coming aboard. Just a few days ago, a shipment of 2,500 life jackets was loaded onto the ship—more than twice the number needed for the 1,200-man crew. While the men saw that as a routine military screw-up, this new cargo is obviously of a much more serious nature.

The crate is secured onto the hangar deck in the middle of the *Indianapolis.* The cylinder is brought into an empty officer's cabin, where it is lowered onto hinged metal straps that have been welded to the floor. The hinges are closed and padlocked.

"I didn't think we were going to use biological warfare in this war," remarks Captain Charles McVay III, who has been told nothing about the contents of either package. His orders are to transport the material with all due haste across the Pacific. The *Indianapolis* was specially chosen for her size and speed—as a heavy cruiser, she is large enough to carry the heavy package, but also much faster than vessels of greater tonnage. Yet McVay has been given very specific instructions: No one must go near them except the two Manhattan Project scientists on board and the marine guards who will stand watch day and night. If the ship should sink, these packages should be placed in a lifeboat and saved at all costs. If the *Indianapolis* comes under attack and is in the unlikely danger of being boarded by the enemy, McVay is to jettison everything overboard to keep it out of Japanese hands.

McVay knows better than to ask questions.

Four hours later, at 8:00 A.M., the *Indianapolis* sails from her berth at Hunter's Point, the naval shipyard in San Francisco. By 8:36 A.M., she passes beneath the Golden Gate Bridge and then beside the Marin Headlands, out to sea. Her first stop is Pearl Harbor, Hawaii, where she will deposit the few passengers now catching a lift to the war zone.

After that, the *Indianapolis* will return to sea.

Next stop: Tinian Island.

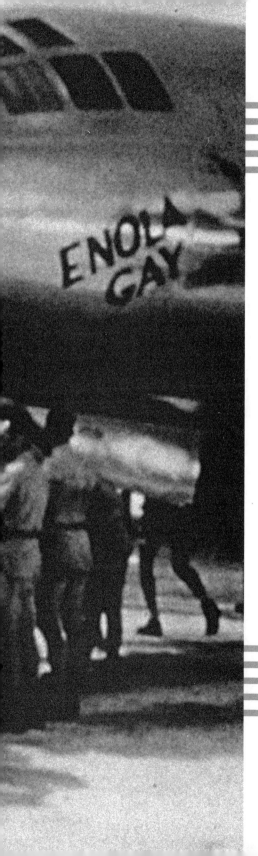

Part Two

"Destination: Hiroshima"

CHAPTER 20

GROUND ZERO
JORNADA DEL MUERTO DESERT
NEW MEXICO

July 16, 1945

B ECAUSE OF THE SUCCESSFUL Trinity test, scientists now believe that the A-bomb material being shipped across the Pacific will produce the explosive force of nineteen thousand tons of dynamite. In addition to the atomic bomb tested in New Mexico, American scientists have built two others. One of them, called Little Boy, is now aboard the *Indianapolis*; the plutonium core of the other is just days away from being flown to the island of Tinian. Neither bomb is yet armed.

Robert Oppenheimer and his crew have discovered that a great fireball will shoot to a height of over forty thousand feet, sucking

Trinitite (also referred to as Atomsite or Alamogordo glass) is thought to have been formed when soil vaporized by the atomic blast rained down as molten droplets and solidified. [National Archives]

up clouds of dust as it ascends. Even as the giant flames faded, northward winds in New Mexico carried radioactive dust across the desert. Alarmingly, the herds of cattle grazing just beyond the blast zone will soon suffer the loss of their hair, indicating that radiation levels around the site are a threat to human life.

Back at ground zero, the steel tower on which the gadget was perched is gone, completely vaporized. There is not much of a crater; instead, the blast has traveled up and out from the ground. For a quarter-mile around the blast site, the earth is scorched black.

The extreme heat has melted the sand into green glass, a material soon to be known as Trinitite.

Of course, such an enormous explosion and burst of light did not go unnoticed. Answering inquiries, the military responds that an ammunition dump at Alamogordo Army Air Field had caught fire.

However, those who can tell the difference between a simple explosion and an earthshaking bang of epic proportions find this difficult to believe. In New Mexico and Texas, newspapers immediately publish stories speculating about what happened. As far away as California, radio broadcasts wonder about the strange events in the New Mexico desert. News spreads up the coast to the state of Washington, where employees at the Hanford Engineer Works quickly deduce that an A-bomb has been detonated. Like Los Alamos, Hanford is a top secret Manhattan Project facility, charged with manufacturing plutonium, a vital ingredient in a nuclear explosion.

CHAPTER 21

BERLIN, GERMANY

July 16, 1945 • 4:00 P.M.

HARRY TRUMAN LOOKS OUT over a most amazing sight: the entire American Second Armored Division standing in formation, awaiting his review. Soldiers, half-tracks, and battle-tested Sherman tanks line the German autobahn just outside Berlin, the olive-drab uniforms of American soldiers stretching as far as the eye can see.

He now plans to spend the afternoon exploring bombed-out Berlin. But first, the president will enjoy the great privilege of reviewing his conquering army. An old soldier himself, Truman clambers out of his presidential limousine and stands atop a half-track where the crowd can see him.

As the vehicle drives slowly past the troops, Truman is overwhelmed at this display of power. The Second is said to be the

Soviet Premier Joseph Stalin, U.S. President Harry S. Truman, and British Prime Minister Winston Churchill at the Potsdam conference, July 17, 1945. [National Archives]

largest armored division on earth, a force that has seen action in North Africa, Sicily, Normandy, and the Battle of the Bulge. It was the first American unit to enter Berlin after the German surrender two months ago.

Yet as President Harry Truman looks down into the faces of these brave men—many of them just a year out of high school—he knows that the Second Armored's war may not be over. Already, one million men comprising thirty divisions are making their way around the world to fight the Japanese. It might be only a matter of weeks until the men of the Second board troop ships heading for the Pacific.

That is, unless Harry Truman can find another way to persuade the Japanese to accept unconditional surrender.

● ● ●

At almost 8:00 P.M., more than six hours after the Trinity detonation, Secretary of War Henry Stimson hands Truman a coded telegram announcing its success. "Operated on this morning. Diagnosis not yet complete but results seem satisfactory and already exceed expectations."

Harry Truman's reaction to the news is guarded, pending specifics about the breadth of the blast. In truth, the president is a mere observer of whatever comes next with the A-bomb. He came to the party late, years after FDR foresaw the potential for a nuclear weapon and approved the Manhattan Project. A former World War I artillery officer, Truman sees the bomb as a weapon of war, one with far greater killing capacity than a tank or a missile, but a conventional weapon nonetheless. While he realizes the war's equation has changed in his favor, he does not yet grasp that Trinity is not just a bomb test but also a split-second explosion that has changed the future of mankind. From this day forward, any nation, no matter how small, in possession of a nuclear device can unleash the bowels of hell any time it wishes.

As for sharing the news about Trinity with Joseph Stalin, wherever he might be, that can wait.

CHAPTER 22

KURE, JAPAN

July 16, 1945

THIS PORT CITY IS IN RUINS. Three weeks ago, 162 American B-29 bombers laid siege to Kure, sinking two submarines still under construction and heavily damaging another. Another bombing followed two weeks ago.

Now, American B-29s have begun dropping mines across the entrance to Japan's great ports, closing every harbor on the Pacific and a great number on the Sea of Japan. The mine campaign will effectively isolate the nation from the rest of the world.

It is not just the heavy bombers of the Army Air Forces that are punishing Japan. Beginning six days ago, on July 10, the U.S. Navy

This illustration of Okinawa, the "Key to Japan," whose capital, Naha, had just been captured by the Americans, was published in the Illustrated London News *on May 26, 1945.* [Mary Evans Picture Library]

OKINAWA ISLAND, THE "KEY TO JAPAN," WHOSE CAPITAL, NAHA, HAS FALLEN.

Drawn by our Special Artist, G. H. Davis.

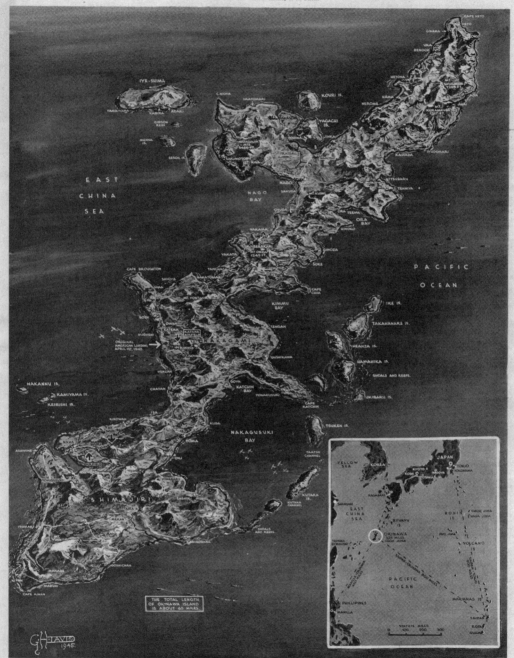

A PICTORIAL MAP OF OKINAWA, VITAL BASE FOR AIR WAR ON JAPAN. (INSET) ITS STRATEGIC SITUATION.

In the largest Pacific amphibious operation to date, men of the U.S. Tenth Army landed on Okinawa, in the Ryukyu Islands, on April 1, after previously capturing islands in the Kerama group to the west. Okinawa, a vital stepping-stone in the Allied advance to Japan herself, lies only 325 miles south-west of Kyushu, and from its air bases all Japan is vulnerable from the air. The conquest of this long and narrow island has not been an easy job for the U.S. troops, for large Japanese forces defended it from rocky heights and fighting from caves, but on May 17 its capital, Naha, was reported to have fallen to General Buckner's soldiers and marines, who stemmed the bloodiest enemy counter-attack of the whole campaign, vainly launched to avert defeat. The battle for Okinawa is vital, the most vital, so far, in the Pacific, for the Allies and for Japan, hence her desperate resistance. In attacks on the other Ryukyus the British Pacific Fleet is playing an important part. A number of our warships have taken blows from Jap suicide aeroplanes, and more than once Admiral Nimitz, usually sparing in his praise, has complimented the British task force.

B-29s drop incendiary bombs on Japan. As many as one thousand planes were in the air when the Allies bombed Tokyo. [Mary Evans Picture Library]

launched a steady stream of aerial attacks by aircraft-carrier–based planes. Naval aviators are now flying hundreds of sorties a day over the Japanese mainland, destroying the nation's shipping, railways, and limited aerial defenses. Unlike the behemoth silver B-29s that

drop their payload from thousands of feet in the air, many of these planes fly so low that the Japanese people actually duck as the fighter-bombers thunder overhead. Often they can clearly see the pilots' faces.

American power is slowly crushing Japan's national morale. A cruel blow came just two days ago: eight ferries carrying coal from the island of Hokkaido to Honshu were sunk, with great loss of life. This leaves Japan with few large vessels to transport coal from the mines of Hokkaido to the Japanese factories that rely on it for power to run their machinery. Without factories, there can be no bombs, guns, planes, or tanks to fuel the Japanese war effort.

Yet even if the factories could find another energy source, production is all but finished. Industrial leaders are now informing Japan's military leaders that they can produce weaponry "for just a few days more" for lack of raw material.

The psychological toll on the Japanese people is also a liability, yet they represent the nation's last chance for a proper defense of the homeland. Hungry, homeless, and increasingly humiliated, the populace is now being ordered to adopt the suicidal *Ketsu-Go* strategy—that is, all Japanese men, women, and children will fight to the death.

For some Japanese soldiers in the distant battlefields of Asia, it is too late for *Ketsu-Go*. They see for themselves that the tide of war has turned. For the first time ever, many Japanese have begun to surrender—mainly because their weapons have been destroyed.

"From May onwards prisoners in a terrible state came in daily, many of them armed with nothing more dangerous than bamboo spears, and trembling with a mixture of malaria and humiliation," one British soldier in Burma will report.

The Japanese war effort is almost on life support.

Japanese prisoners of war are searched by American soldiers. This photo was likely taken in the Philippines.
[Library of Congress]

CHAPTER 23

POTSDAM, GERMANY

July 25, 1945 • Late evening

PRESIDENT HARRY TRUMAN IS HOMESICK. On the road for almost two weeks, he has maintained his normal routine of rising early and enjoying a breakfast of oatmeal, orange juice, toast, and milk. Yet he misses his wife, Bess, and the things that make a home a home, like his favorite White House dinner of chicken and dumplings. But right now food is not on Truman's mind. He is immersed in his journal, penning his notes on the Potsdam conference. The reports of Trinity's power have disturbed him, allowing the president to see at last that America possesses an unparalleled weapon of war.

"We have discovered the most terrible formula in the history of the world," Truman writes. "It may be the fire destruction prophesied in the Euphrates Valley Era, after Noah and his fabulous Ark."

The words flow quickly onto the page, but each is chosen with care. For good or bad, Truman knows that history will long judge this journal entry. It was only yesterday that he authorized the dropping of atomic bombs on Japan.

After conferring with his military advisers and with Winston Churchill in Potsdam just before noon on July 24, 1945, Truman has allowed the process to move forward. It was a fairly easy decision, despite the objections of some nuclear scientists at Los Alamos and even General Dwight Eisenhower, Truman's top commander in Europe, who believes that Japan is close to surrendering. In the end, Truman came to the conclusion that an invasion would cost too many American lives.

"The final decision of where and when to use the atomic bomb was up to me. Let there be no mistake about it," Truman will later write, but the truth is that the decision was made long ago by Franklin Roosevelt, who had no qualms whatsoever about the prospect of using the atomic bomb. FDR was so fed up with the death and destruction in Europe and the Pacific that he had little hesitation in authorizing the two-billion-dollar Manhattan Project.

Nonetheless, Truman is the one man in the world with the power to stop the bombing of Japan, and he chooses not to do so. He issues no verbal or written order to announce his decision. Truman does nothing more than get out of the way; what will happen, will happen. It is a rare display of passive behavior by a man so prone to action, but his thinking is clear.

It is late in the night as Truman continues his journal entry in

President Truman's motorcade drives past units of the Second Armored Division on the autobahn between Potsdam and Berlin, Germany. President Truman is in the area to attend the Potsdam conference. [National Archives]

The last meeting of the Potsdam conference. President Truman, wearing glasses, is on the right side of the photograph; Soviet Premier Joseph Stalin, in a white uniform, is at the top. Newly elected British Prime Minister Clement Attlee, who replaced Winston Churchill, sits at the lower left, five chairs over from both Truman and Stalin. [National Archives]

Potsdam: "This weapon is to be used against Japan between now and August 10th. I have told the Sec. of War, Mr. Stimson, to use it so that military objectives and soldiers and sailors are the target, not women and children. Even if the Japs are savages, ruthless, merciless and fanatic, we as the leader of the world for the common welfare cannot drop this terrible bomb on the old Capitol or the new."

The decision to spare the modern capital of Tokyo and the nearby port of Yokohama, along with the ancient capital of Kyoto, has made it almost inevitable that Hiroshima will be attacked first. The waterfront city of 350,000 has not once been firebombed, making it a prime unscathed target. Many of its residents are Japanese soldiers and marines; the port itself is one of the nation's largest military supply depots. Truman's insistence on military targets makes Hiroshima a natural bull's-eye for the bomb that has just reached the island of Tinian and is being unloaded from the USS *Indianapolis* at this very moment.

And with Truman's refusal to destroy Kyoto, the city of Nagasaki is added to the target list in its place.

"The target will be a purely military one and we will issue a warning statement asking the Japs to surrender and save lives," Truman writes. "I'm sure they will not do that, but we will have given them the chance. It is certainly a good thing for the world that Hitler's crowd or Stalin's did not discover this atomic bomb. It seems to be the most terrible thing ever discovered, but it can be made the most useful."

Truman's concern about Stalin is very real. The Soviet Union's approach to the shape of the postwar world is to relentlessly demand more control over territories it has seized in Europe. The United States' position is to oppose Soviet expansion.

The Soviets now have more than one million men on the Manchurian border, poised to attack Japanese occupying forces. The presence of such a large force in China means that the Soviets will soon want a considerable say in the future of Asia. It is a tiresome negotiation, yet Truman has stood up to the Soviets time and again, refusing to allow Stalin to occupy more territory.

The ornate great hall of the Cecilienhof Palace is sweltering. For reasons of decorum, the president will not remove his double-breasted suit coat or even loosen his bow tie. Throughout the afternoon, fifteen leaders and diplomats sit around the ten-foot-wide circular conference table, with Joseph Stalin to Truman's far right.

This summit marks the first time Truman and Stalin have met in person. Over the course of the negotiations, the president has been uncowed by the Soviet leader, who prefers to wear a military uniform and answers most questions with a simple grunt. This habit amuses Truman, even though he is well aware of Stalin's barbarity.

Shortly before 5:00 P.M. the meeting ends. At the conclusion of a long afternoon around the bargaining table, Truman rises from his seat and walks five chairs to his right, where Stalin stands to stretch his legs. Casually, so as not to alarm the Soviet leader,

Truman quietly informs Stalin that the United States has "a new weapon of unusual destructive force."

Stalin pauses, then speaks through his interpreter: "I am glad to hear it. I hope you will make good use of it against the Japanese," the Soviet dictator says—and makes his exit.

Almost immediately, Truman is confronted by Churchill, who is confused. The men can't believe Stalin is so indifferent.

In fact, Joseph Stalin is panicked. He is a man for whom total power is everything, and the idea that his military might could be diminished is intolerable. Joseph Stalin has murdered millions of his own citizens and has allowed his troops to loot and pillage Germany and Eastern Europe. His goal is to dominate the world. He is terrified that this new weapon will shift the balance of power in favor of the Americans.

After leaving the great hall of Cecilienhof Palace, Stalin quickly dictates a telegram to the scientists at work on Russia's own nuclear program: "Hurry with the job."

CHAPTER 24

MANILA CITY HALL
MANILA, PHILIPPINES

July 30, 1945 • 3:15 P.M.

T HE MOST POWERFUL MAN in the Pacific has no idea that the atomic bomb is operational and that massive destruction is just days away.

At the Potsdam conference, President Truman's military advisers now know about Trinity, as do Britain's and the Soviet Union's top generals.

In Germany, General Dwight Eisenhower, commander of all Allied forces in Europe, was informed of the nuclear weapon's success over dinner one week ago. "They told me they were going to drop it on the Japanese," Eisenhower will later state. "I was against it on two counts. First, the Japanese were ready to surrender and it

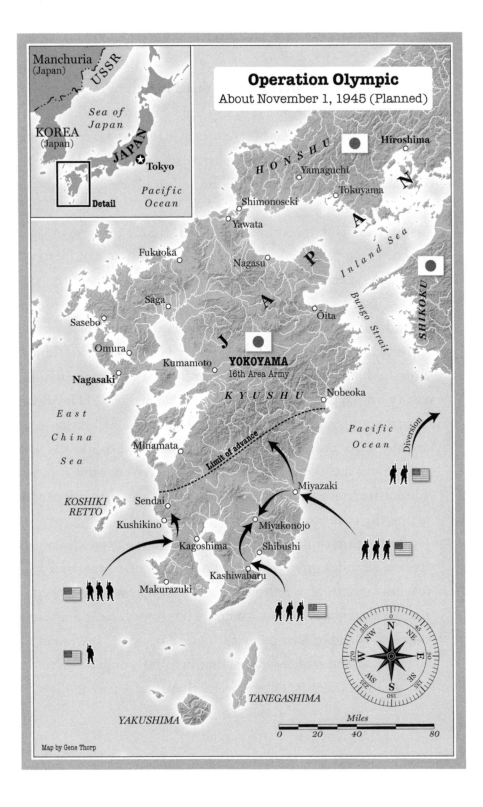

Operation Olympic

About November 1, 1945 (Planned)

Manchuria
(Japan)

USSR

KOREA
(Japan)

Sea of
Japan

JAPAN

Tokyo

Pacific
Ocean

Detail

HONSHU

Hiroshima

Yamaguchi

Tokuyama

Shimonoseki

Yawata

JAPAN

Fukuoka

Nagasu

Inland Sea

SHIKOKU

Saga

Oita

Bungo Strait

Sasebo

Omura

YOKOYAMA
16th Area Army

Nagasaki

Kumamoto

KYUSHU

Nobeoka

East
China
Sea

Minamata

Limit of advance

Pacific
Ocean

Diversion

KOSHIKI
RETTO

Sendai

Miyazaki

Kushikino

Kagoshima

Miyakonojo

Shibushi

Makurazuki

Kashiwabaru

TANEGASHIMA

N
NW   NE
W   E
SW   SE
S

YAKUSHIMA

Miles
0   20   40   80

Map by Gene Thorp

wasn't necessary to hit them with that awful thing. Second, I hate to see our country being the first to use such a weapon."

But General Douglas MacArthur, a man who has served under eight presidents, who has been awarded a Medal of Honor and commands more than one million fighting men, has been told nothing.

Even as his staff continues to prepare for the invasion of Japan, an event Douglas MacArthur believes will result in "a million casualties," the general lives a life of leisure.

On this sweltering Monday afternoon, a delegation fills his second-floor office at command headquarters. The guests include General Counsel of the Navy H. Struve Hensel and Vice Admiral Ross T. McIntire, who until very recently served as Franklin Roosevelt's personal physician. Their manner is deferential, befitting the respect due a commander of MacArthur's stature. While his guests remain seated, the general paces the room and thinks out loud throughout their visit, as is his custom. MacArthur's top staff, who admire him tremendously, sometimes mimic this behavior to add a little levity to their day.

As the thirty-minute meeting winds to a polite conclusion and the five-man delegation is ushered out the door, MacArthur has a few brief moments to reflect on the shocking news that landed on his desk yesterday: Japanese troops are pouring onto the mainland's southern island of Kyushu, with "no end in sight." Instead of the eighty thousand soldiers MacArthur believed would be defending the invasion beaches, he will learn that nine Japanese divisions comprising more than five hundred thousand men are now digging in on the coastline, waiting for the Americans to land. Almost all are stationed at Kyushu's southern beaches, the site of MacArthur's invasion, Operation Olympic.

He knows this because American forces captured Japanese

This machine deciphered the Japanese "Purple" code used to send messages to diplomats and military leaders in London, Washington, and Berlin. It took the Allies two years to break the code. [National Archives]

codebooks during the battles for Iwo Jima and Okinawa, allowing intelligence units based in Pearl Harbor to read top secret enemy documents. Operation Magic is the code name for the program that decrypts Japanese messages; the men who decode them call themselves magicians.

MacArthur is troubled. Allied forces now control most of the Pacific, but the Japanese still own much of Asia's Pacific Rim. Their air force bases in Korea, China, and northern Japan will allow them to launch kamikaze aircraft against an invasion fleet. In addition, the Imperial Japanese Navy's Twelfth Flotilla, based on Kyushu, has nine hundred hidden planes that will be utilized for suicide flights. Vintage wooden biplanes, invisible to American radar, are also being retrofitted for nighttime suicide attacks.

Just as menacing, employees at the Sasebo Naval Station near Nagasaki are working double shifts to build special suicide boats designed to ram landing craft laden with U.S. soldiers. The Japanese believe they know precisely where American troops will invade, so vast underground caves are being constructed behind the beaches and stocked with food and ammunition. All civilians are being forcibly removed from the southward-facing coastal regions so that barbed wire, artillery batteries, mines, and antitank defenses can be installed and camouflaged.

He realizes that the enemy is "changing the tactical and strategic situation sharply." No longer will the Japanese utilize the *fukkaku* strategy employed on Peleliu, Iwo Jima, and Okinawa, lying in wait to repel the American attack from hidden defensive bunkers. Now it is clear to MacArthur that they will defend the beaches with even more fury than the Germans showed during the D-Day landing in France. The sands of Kyushu could very well become an American graveyard.

To MacArthur's way of thinking, there are three ways for America to knock out Japan: a naval blockade followed by an invasion; a naval blockade followed by massive aerial bombing; or a straight-up beach invasion. As an army officer and a general committed to

Young Japanese kamikaze pilots receive a drink at a farewell ceremony before their suicide missions, 1944.
[Mary Evans Picture Library]

commanding the largest military force in history, MacArthur refuses to concede that naval and air forces should determine the outcome of the war. Paranoid by nature and creating conflicts where they might not otherwise exist, MacArthur thinks the other two services are aligned in a conspiracy to prevent his army from getting the glory.

Foolishly, MacArthur is openly antagonistic to Admiral Chester Nimitz, his naval equal in rank and power, calling his tactical strategies "just awful." The navy, MacArthur believes, wants to "control all overseas positions after the war, using the Marines, and using the Army as a sort of home guard."

Nonetheless, he needs the sailors and flyboys. His invasion needs air support, called Operation Coronet in the plans. The cornerstones of Operation Olympic are the ongoing preinvasion aerial bombardment of Japan's industrial sector and the obliteration of Japan's navy by the ships and planes of a U.S. Navy carrier task force. After that, MacArthur's Sixth Army will deliver the decisive blow with its landing on Kyushu.

The general has confided in friends that he believes the Japanese will surrender by September 1, but reports indicate that the enemy is spoiling for a fight.

The timing of Operation Olympic is also in grave danger. An invasion is more than just the act of sending men ashore; soldiers need to be fed, armed, and cared for in case of injury. MacArthur is awaiting the arrival of troops from Europe as well as stockpiling weapons, ammunition, landing vessels, food, and hospital supplies. He cannot attack for four to five months at the earliest, giving the Japanese even more time to prepare.

The confident tone of other recently intercepted Japanese communiqués makes one thing certain: the enemy's determination to slaughter Americans will only increase during this lull.

Hundreds of ships of the U.S. fleet gather at Ulithi Atoll in the Caroline Islands to prepare for a preinvasion bombardment of Japan. Foreground to background are the aircraft carriers USS Wasp, *USS* Yorktown, *USS* Hornet, *USS* Hancock, *USS* Ticonderoga, *and USS* Lexington. [National Archives]

CHAPTER 25

MANILA, PHILIPPINES

August 1, 1945

ENERAL CARL "TOOEY" SPAATZ arrives in Manila to meet with General Douglas MacArthur. The newly appointed commander of U.S. Strategic Air Forces in the Pacific has been flying for most of the last five days, traveling 8,500 miles from Washington, D.C., to Honolulu to Guam and on to Manila. Spaatz is here not of his own volition but because he was ordered to brief MacArthur by General Thomas Handy, acting as army chief of staff while General George Marshall was in Potsdam with the president.

A man of average height, the fifty-four-year-old Spaatz was present in Reims, France, when the Germans surrendered on May 7, 1945, and is now posted to the Pacific to facilitate a similar situation with the Japanese. But his first order of business will be ensuring the deployment of the atomic bomb. Handy gave Spaatz the order verbally, but Spaatz refused to take the assignment unless given instructions in writing. "Listen, Tom," Spaatz told Handy, aware that he could be tried for war crimes if held personally liable for the loss of life that will ensue. "If I'm going to kill 100,000 people, I'm not going to do it on verbal orders. I want a piece of paper."

Handy protested that putting such an order in writing compromised security. Even Harry Truman has refused to affix his signature to any order connecting him with the dropping of the A-bomb. But Spaatz insisted. Finally, Handy caved. "I guess I agree, Tooey," the acting chief of staff admitted. "If a fellow thinks he might blow up the whole end of Japan, he ought to have a piece of paper."

Handy signed the order, but it was actually written by General Leslie Groves of the Manhattan Project.

It is, perhaps, the most important directive in world history.

General Spaatz wants MacArthur to know about the atomic bomb before it is dropped. As Groves later comments, "If the weather had been suitable, the bomb would have been dropped before MacArthur had ever been informed by Spaatz, which would have been quite surprising."

Spaatz, a man known for his curt speech pattern and matter-of-fact planning, is weary as he greets MacArthur. For a moment the two men speak casually. Spaatz is not used to the tropical heat; he sweats through his uniform. And yet the weight of what he must tell the general compels him so much that he cannot rest until he hands MacArthur the A-bomb order.

"I didn't try to explain it," Spaatz will later recall. "I just handed it to him and thought that he would ask me lots of questions, but instead he talked about that letter for about five minutes and the rest of the hour proceeded to expound the theories of atomic energy to me."

The order begins specifically: the first "special bomb" will be dropped as soon after August 3, 1945, as weather will permit visual bombing on one of the targets: Hiroshima, Kokura, Niigata, or Nagasaki.

Secondly: "Additional bombs will be delivered on the above targets as soon as made ready by the project staff. Further instructions will be issued concerning targets other than those listed above."

The third clause is a warning: "Dissemination of any and all information concerning the use of the weapon against Japan is reserved to the Secretary of War and the President of the United States. No communiques on the subject or releases of information will be issued by Commanders in the field without specific prior authority. Any news stories will be sent to the War Department for special clearance."

The final directive of the order is specifically targeted at Spaatz: "It is desired that you personally deliver one copy of this directive to General MacArthur and one copy to Admiral Nimitz for their information."

Nimitz, whose Pacific Fleet is headquartered in Guam, has already read the order.

So it is that General Douglas MacArthur is the last to know

about Japan's doom. He scribbles his initials—"MACA"—in the right margin to verify that he has received the one-page document.

General MacArthur is not alone among United States military leaders in initially opposing the bomb. Generals Hap Arnold and Dwight Eisenhower have objected in top secret circles, as have Admiral William D. Leahy, Rear Admiral Lewis L. Strauss, Assistant Secretary of War John J. McCloy, and Assistant Secretary of the Navy Ralph A. Bard. The consensus of these men is that the atomic bomb is too destructive and too many civilians will be killed.

Those in favor of the A-bomb attack, such as Secretary of War Henry Stimson and the U.S. Army chief of staff, General George C. Marshall, are more closely tied to the White House than to actual combat operations in the field.

But MacArthur's displeasure runs much deeper than that of the other dissenters.

The general is a brilliant tactician. He also has a deep understanding of Japanese culture, believing that the nation will never completely surrender and cooperate with an ensuing national occupation unless Emperor Hirohito is allowed to remain in power after the war ends.

But there is a harsher truth.

MacArthur is so determined to command Operation Olympic that he downplays projected casualties in communications with Marshall. In a cable to the general, meant for the eyes of President Harry Truman, he assured them that losses would be less than a hundred thousand men.

"Your message arrived with thirty minutes to spare," Marshall cabled back to MacArthur, "and had determining influence in obtaining formal presidential approval for Olympic."

But now, Operation Olympic will never happen. Douglas MacArthur understands that his dream of conquering the nation of Japan by leading a ground invasion is over.

This is a cruel blow for MacArthur. Convinced of his own military genius, MacArthur has openly disparaged fellow army generals Dwight Eisenhower and George Patton, stating that they "made every mistake that supposedly intelligent men could make." In an interview with the *New York Herald Tribune* in November 1944, MacArthur went on to say, "The European strategy was to hammer stupidly against the enemy's strongest points." With "just a portion of the force" given to Patton in North Africa, MacArthur bragged, he "could have retaken the Philippines in three months."

General Douglas MacArthur does not want to bomb the Japanese—he wants to crush them up close and personal.

To his mind, that kind of victory would make him immortal.

CHAPTER 26

HIROSHIMA, JAPAN

August 3, 1945 • 7:30 A.M.

THE ANGRY DRONE OF B-29 bomber engines is not an unusual sound for the people of this densely populated port city. On a heavily overcast morning, air-raid sirens once again announce the arrival of the silver behemoths, thundering overhead unopposed at an elevation of twenty thousand feet. Since Hiroshima has not been bombed during the war, most citizens think the sirens are just another false alarm. There is no stampede to take refuge in the bomb shelters.

But this raid is different. It is rush hour in Hiroshima, and as commuters on their way to work by streetcar, bicycle, and bus can clearly see, bombs are tumbling out of the warplanes, soon to inflict the same horrific damage on Hiroshima that has been visited on almost every other major city in Japan.

Pre-attack mosaic view—marked SECRET—of Hiroshima, Japan. This image is made up of many smaller images that fit together to give a picture of the area. [National Archives]

PRE - ATTACK MOSAIC
(UNCONTROLLED)
HIROSHIMA
PHOTOS OF 13 APRIL 1945

0   2000   4000
     1000   3000   5000
              FEET

PHOTO I - II (PS)   SECRET

SECRET

Until today, this city located on the Ota River delta has been spared, even as B-29 raids have systematically destroyed most of Japan. Major cities like Tokyo were bombed first. Now General Curtis LeMay is directing his bombers toward secondary targets, such as Toyama, a hub for ball-bearing and aluminum production. Two days ago, 173 B-29s literally leveled Toyama by dropping 1,466 tons of conventional and incendiary bombs on the city. No home or industry was left undamaged, with one estimate showing 99.5 percent of Toyama wiped off the map.

The August 1 attacks focused on Japan's ability to transport men and matériel. The Army Air Forces' Fifty-Eighth Bomb Wing obliterated the rail hub of Hachioji. The 313th Bomb Wing decimated the rail hub of Nagaoka, and the 314th vaporized the tiny rail center of Mito.

Since the Tokyo firebombings in March, the full scope of LeMay's aerial attacks has emerged: One million Japanese have died or been wounded in sixty-six targeted cities. Ten million more have been made homeless.

But as the B-29s open their bomb bay doors over Hiroshima this morning, it is not fire that falls from the sky. Instead, unarmed five-hundred-pound canisters hurtle toward the ground. At four thousand feet, an altitude charge automatically opens them. Hundreds of thousands of four-by-eight-inch slips of paper, the LeMay bombing leaflets, are released into the sky and flutter to the ground.

"Civilians!" they read in Japanese. "Evacuate at once!

"These leaflets are being dropped to notify you that your city has been listed for destruction by our powerful air force. The bombing will begin within seventy-two hours.

"This advance notice will give your military authorities ample time to take necessary defensive measures to protect you from our inevitable attack. Watch and see how powerless they are to protect you. Systematic destruction of city after city will continue as long as you blindly follow your military leaders whose blunders have placed you on the very brink of oblivion. It is your responsibility to overthrow the military government now and save what is left of your beautiful country.

"In the meanwhile, we encourage all civilians to evacuate at once."

One week ago at the Potsdam conference, President Harry Truman issued a simple warning that if Japan did not surrender immediately, it would face "prompt and utter destruction." It was the

Thousands of these leaflets were dropped from B-29s over Japan to warn that cities would be bombed to total destruction. [Los Alamos National Laboratory]

last line of the Potsdam Declaration, a joint proclamation by the United States, Great Britain, and China defining the terms for Japanese surrender. Many citizens throughout Japan know of this ultimatum because American radio broadcasts have delivered it in Japanese.

As the leaflets reach the ground, the people of Hiroshima open them to see aerial photographs of five B-29s unleashing scores of bombs on Japan. Circles line the bottom, each representing a city that has been targeted. B-29s have been dropping these leaflets on cities all over Japan for more than a week.

By any estimate, Hiroshima is a perfect target. Japanese authorities are so convinced of this that they have already evacuated almost a hundred thousand citizens to safer locations.

Hiroshima is entirely flat and just a few feet above sea level, meaning that an explosion will expand outward with maximum effect. The city is also the headquarters of Japan's Second Army, whose twenty-five thousand soldiers will be vital to thwarting an American invasion. In addition, Hiroshima possesses a massive armament storage depot. It is a thriving port and communications hub.

As American B-29s pass over the city, then out over the Sea of Japan, and return to their bases in the Mariana Islands six hours away, the people of Hiroshima are left to wonder what the leaflets really mean.

CHAPTER 27

TINIAN, MARIANA ISLANDS

August 3, 1945

O N THE ISLAND OF TINIAN, 1,500 miles southeast of Hiroshima, final preparations for the dropping of the atomic bomb are in place. Today might have seen the B-29 crews release the bomb known as Little Boy instead of warning leaflets. But a typhoon approaching Japan made flying conditions less than ideal.

Little Boy has been ready to go for three days. The five-ton explosive device rests on a special trailer, covered in canvas to conceal its appearance. All Little Boy lacks to be activated are the four cordite charges that will initiate the explosion. These will not be secured in the bomb until the B-29 carrying it to Hiroshima has taken off, just in case the plane crashes on the runway.

The pilot flying the bombing mission is Colonel Paul W. Tibbets,

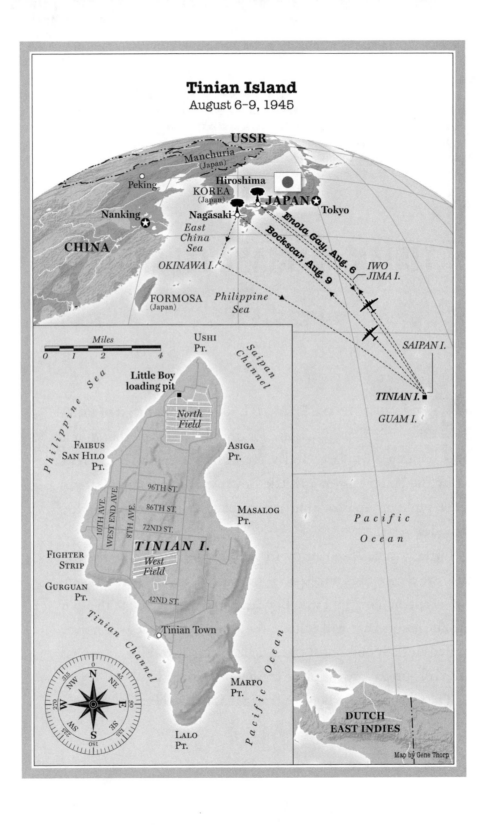

Tinian Island
August 6-9, 1945

USSR

Manchuria (Japan)

Peking

Hiroshima

KOREA (Japan)

JAPAN Tokyo

Nagasaki

East China Sea

Nanking

CHINA

OKINAWA I.

FORMOSA (Japan)

Philippine Sea

Enola Gay, Aug. 6

Bockscar, Aug. 9

IWO JIMA I.

SAIPAN I.

TINIAN I.

GUAM I.

Miles

0 1 2 4

USHI PT.

Saipan Channel

Little Boy loading pit

North Field

Philippine Sea

FAIBUS SAN HILO PT.

ASIGA PT.

96TH ST.

86TH ST.

72ND ST.

10TH AVE.

WEST END AVE.

8TH AVE.

MASALOG PT.

TINIAN I.

West Field

Pacific Ocean

FIGHTER STRIP

GURGUAN PT.

42ND ST.

Tinian Town

Tinian Channel

MARPO PT.

N
NW NE
W E
SW SE
S

Pacific Ocean

LALO PT.

DUTCH EAST INDIES

Map by Gene Thorp

a thirty-year-old career officer who was born in Quincy, Illinois. Tibbets has flown forty-three combat missions over German-occupied Europe and North Africa. He has been flying the B-29 since its debut in 1943. At this moment, the aircraft he will fly has no catchy name, no artwork emblazoned across its nose. Right now, it is known only by the number painted on its fuselage: 82.

Tibbets was personally selected by General Leslie Groves to lead the elite detachment of pilots who will drop atomic weapons on Japan. He has been practicing the bombing for weeks, flying out over the Pacific with a dummy version of Little Boy and dropping it in the ocean. Now Tibbets is waiting on the weather. The skies have to be clear enough over Hiroshima to visually see the target and deploy the bomb.

The final word will come from General Curtis LeMay, who will inform Washington that he has given the order for Tibbets to take off. "Firm decision is expected at 050400z," reads a top secret telegram to the War Department.

Colonel Tibbets knows it is almost time. "The actual and forecast weather were almost identical," he will later remember.

"So we got busy."

Colonel Paul Tibbets waves from the cockpit of Enola Gay *before takeoff on August 6, 1945.*
[National Archives]

CHAPTER 28

IMPERIAL PALACE TOKYO, JAPAN

August 3, 1945

I N TOKYO, EMPEROR HIROHITO is not concerned. The words "prompt and utter destruction" delivered by President Harry Truman have not resonated with the emperor. Like his latest prime minister, Kantaro Suzuki, he believes those words to be recycled rhetoric—*yaki naoshi*—from previous meetings among Allied leaders. So he ignores Truman's ultimatum, still believing that the Soviet Union will help broker a peace to his liking with the West—completely oblivious to the fact that Soviet leader Joseph Stalin is just five days away from invading Japanese-held Manchuria.

At a point when Hirohito's nation desperately needs him to

show wisdom and discretion, the emperor is being delusional.

Meanwhile, Hirohito's cabinet and the Supreme Council for the Direction of the War are holding a joint session. The topic of debate is whether or not any surrender is permissible. They have argued the matter for more than a week, with no conclusion in sight.

Like their divine emperor, this group of politicians and military leaders believe that Truman will not follow through on his demand of unconditional surrender. Time, they believe, is on their side. In a statement to the world's media on July 27 the Japanese formally rejected any notion that they will accede to Truman's demands. Later that day, Prime Minister Suzuki holds a press conference to reiterate those sentiments, stating that "the only alternative for us is to be determined to continue our fight to the end."

Mitsumasa Yonai, minister of the Imperial Japanese Navy.
[Mary Evans Picture Library]

Joining their emperor in delusion, the Japanese leadership believe they still control their destiny.

As Navy Minister Mitsumasa Yonai states about Truman's promise of total annihilation: "America is beginning to be isolated. The government therefore will ignore it.

"There is no need to rush."

CHAPTER 29

NORTH FIELD
TINIAN, MARIANA ISLANDS

August 4, 1945 • 3:00 P.M.

CRADLING A KAYWOODIE BRIAR pipe in his left hand, Colonel Tibbets, the commander of America's nuclear strike force, strides past a cordon of armed guards, hurrying into the Quonset hut that will serve as today's briefing room. Tibbets is obsessively punctual, and today is no exception. The meeting is due to start at precisely 3:00 P.M. As he pushes into the crowded room, he is not a second late.

Crews on B-29s average eleven men. Seven aircraft are now being readied for flight. The crewmen, all in lightweight khaki uniforms, sit on hard wooden chairs. Tibbets handpicked these men. All are in their twenties and thirties. They are the best of the best, soon

Captain William Parsons and Colonel Tibbets on Tinian Island. Parsons said, "The bomb you are about to drop is something new in the history of warfare." [Los Alamos National Laboratory]

to fly a world-changing mission over what they refer to as "the Empire."

Tibbets does not mince words. "The moment has arrived. This is what we have all been working towards. Very recently the weapon we are about to deliver was successfully tested in the States. We have received orders to drop it on the enemy."

Behind Tibbets are two blackboards covered by thick cloth. Two intelligence officers step forward and remove the drapes, revealing maps of Hiroshima, Kokura, and Nagasaki. Tibbets states that these are the targets. He then breaks down each crew's responsibilities: Lieutenant Charles McKnight, in the B-29 named *Big Stink*, will fly to Iwo Jima and remain there as a backup in case of emergency; Captain Ralph Taylor Jr.'s *Full House*, Captain Claude Eatherly's *Straight Flush*, and Captain John Wilson's *Jabit III* will fly an hour ahead over the targets to report on the weather; *Necessary Evil*, piloted by Captain George Marquardt, will photograph the explosion; and Major Charles Sweeney's *The Great Artiste* will measure the blast by dropping scientific instruments that will float to the ground by parachute and radio details back to Guam and Tinian.

Tibbets will pilot the plane containing the A-bomb.

Since the 509th Composite Group was activated in December 1944, these crews have trained in utter secrecy. They

An aerial view of the North Field at the air base on Tinian, where B-29s are ready to fly. [National Archives]

are not popular here in Tinian, where other bomber squadrons mock their many privileges and top secret compound. But they ignore the taunts, knowing they have been training for a high-level mission that could end the war. To prepare, Tibbets was given fifteen B-29s and a top secret training location in the Utah desert. Once the crews Tibbets handpicked flew to Tinian a month ago,

Little Boy just before being lifted into Enola Gay. [Los Alamos National Laboratory]

they began simulating a unique sort of bombing mission: instead of dozens of bombs, they practiced dropping just one rotund "pumpkin bomb." At five tons, nearly eleven feet in length, and five feet in diameter, the pumpkin bomb approximated the size of the atomic bomb known as Fat Man. This allowed pilots to get a feel for how the actual bomb would fall as it is deployed from their forward bomb bay.

Little Boy is a different shape from Fat Man, measuring ten feet long and just a bit more than two feet in diameter. The men of the 509th successfully drop-tested a nonatomic replica of Little Boy on July 23.

Tibbets calls forty-three-year-old navy officer William S. "Deak" Parsons to the platform. An ordnance expert by training, Captain Parsons has served in a most unique capacity during the war, spending much of his time at Los Alamos, where he worked not only with Robert Oppenheimer on the design and development of Little Boy but also with General Groves on the Target Committee. He even observed the Trinity explosion less than a month ago.

Parsons organized all the preparations for Little Boy's delivery to Tinian. It was Parsons who personally met with Captain Charles McVay of the USS *Indianapolis* in San Francisco to convey the order that his ship "will sail at high speed to Tinian."

Throughout his two years in Los Alamos, Captain Parsons's primary motivation for designing the bomb has been to end the war. This ambition became personal shortly after the *Indianapolis* set sail from San Francisco, when Parsons made a rapid detour to see his young half brother in a San Diego naval hospital.

Bob Parsons was among the twenty thousand American casualties during the fierce fighting on Iwo Jima. Once handsome, the Marine Corps private's face is now permanently disfigured: the right side caved in, his jaw gone, a pink prosthesis in the socket where his right eye once rested.

Deak Parsons knows he can do little to help his younger brother, but believes dropping the A-bomb will prevent the same thing from happening to other young American men.

At the podium, Captain Parsons looks at the faces of the aviators gathered in this stuffy Quonset hut and tells them all about the weapon that will win the war.

"The bomb you are about to drop is something new in the history of warfare," Parsons begins. "It is the most destructive weapon ever produced."

Following orders to keep the source of the detonation a secret, he does not use the words "atomic" or "nuclear." Instead, he draws a picture of the enormous mushroom cloud in chalk on a blackboard, describing how the cloud vacuumed sand off the desert floor and carried it thousands of feet into the air.

"We think it will knock out everything within a three-mile area," Parsons tells the men, adding that Little Boy might be even more powerful than the Trinity explosion: "No one knows what will happen when the bomb is dropped from the air."

The B-29 crewmen are stunned. Such a weapon is beyond their comprehension.

Tibbets once again takes his place on the briefing platform.

"Whatever any of us, including myself, has done until now is small potatoes compared to what we are going to do," he is remembered as saying. "I'm proud to be associated with you. Your morale has been high, even though it was difficult not knowing what you were doing, thinking that maybe you were wasting your time, and that the 'gimmick' was just somebody's wild dream.

"I am personally honored—and I'm sure all of you are, too—to take part in this raid which will shorten the war by at least six months."

Tibbets gazes out over the room one last time.

"Depending on the weather, this mission will go off on August sixth."

CHAPTER 30

HIROSHIMA, JAPAN

August 5, 1945

AFTER THE TRINITY A-BOMB test took place in the New Mexico desert three weeks ago, British physicist William Penney of the Manhattan Project measured the blast and reported that another such explosion "would reduce a city of three or four hundred thousand people to nothing but a sink for disaster relief, bandages and hospitals."

The force of the test explosion was equivalent to ten thousand tons of dynamite. A brilliant fireball was followed by a purple cloud glowing with radioactivity that soared into the stratosphere. Everything within the blast zone was vaporized.

If a man had been standing within that zone, he would have died in a fraction of a second, but not before his bone marrow boiled and his flesh literally exploded from his skeleton. In the next millisecond, nothing of that person would remain except compressed gas, which would be instantly sucked up into that great purple cloud racing high into the sky.

The Trinity A-bomb test killed no one. But now a new chapter of warfare is about to begin.

●   ●   ●

Tonight, 588 B-29s are attacking four cities throughout Japan, though Hiroshima will not be one of them. Not a single plane will be shot down. The Americans, it seems, can bomb wherever they want, whenever they want, and whatever they want.

CHAPTER 31

NORTH FIELD
TINIAN, MARIANA ISLANDS

August 5, 1945 • 2:30 P.M.

PREPARATION HAS BEEN INTENSE. At 2:00 P.M., Little Boy was pulled by tractor to a special loading pit. Due to its size, it cannot fit beneath the B-29's fuselage for loading like normal bombs, so a concrete-lined pit has been dug into the earth. At 2:15, the Hiroshima strike plane was backed over the pit before the atomic weapon was loaded into the bomb bay with a hydraulic lift. Captain Deak Parsons entered the bay to practice the eleven steps necessary to arm the bomb midflight, which he has never done before. He is well aware that four B-29s rolling out for standard bombing missions have crashed on takeoff, detonating all their explosives. Parsons is openly fearful that a similar crash will wipe Tinian off the map.

Tibbets finally decides on a nickname for the B-29 with the number 82 painted on the rear of the fuselage. He writes the words on a scrap of paper and hands it to a sign painter in midafternoon. In the past, he has favored aggressive names such as *Butcher Shop* and *Red Gremlin* for his aircraft. But the plane he will fly tonight will hold a special place in history, so he indulges in a rare display of sentiment.

By 4:00 P.M. the aircraft is formally christened *Enola Gay*, in honor of Tibbets's fifty-four-year-old mother. Years ago, when the colonel angered his father by quitting his job as a physician's assistant at a venereal disease clinic to pursue a flying career, it was

Enola Gay *at rest.*
[Los Alamos National Laboratory]

Enola Gay who calmed the waters. "If you want to go kill yourself," his father had said angrily, "I don't give a damn."

To which his mother added quietly, "Paul, if you want to go fly airplanes, you're going to be all right."

Now, with ENOLA GAY painted in block letters just beneath the cockpit, she and her son will forever be linked in history.

By 5:30, the B-29 is ready for preflight testing, which goes off without incident.

At 8:00 P.M., Colonel Tibbets conducts another briefing. In addition to flight routes, altitudes, and departure times, he pinpoints the location of rescue ships and submarines that will be in the area in case a plane must ditch in the ocean. This information is particularly vital because the U.S. Navy has just issued a warning for all ships to stay at least fifty miles away from Hiroshima. This reduces the potential number of rescue vessels, meaning that only a precise water landing will save Tibbets and his crew in an emergency.

Catholic Mass is prayed at 10:00 P.M. A Protestant service follows immediately at 10:30. Almost every man attends one or the other. Tibbets, whose only faith is in the physics of aviation, attends neither. The men are loose but pensive—trained professionals who have flown scores of combat missions. However, during the final preflight meal of sausage, blueberry pancakes, and real eggs in the mess hall after midnight, Tibbets is nervous, though trying not to show it. He eats little, preferring to drink black coffee and smoke his pipe. His time has almost come.

CHAPTER 32

NORTH FIELD
TINIAN, MARIANA ISLANDS

August 6, 1945 • 1:30 A.M.

COLONEL PAUL TIBBETS SITS in the front seat of a six-by-six army truck. Approaching the B-29 he personally selected for this mission, Tibbets wears a one-piece tan flight suit and a billed cap. In preparation for the coming twelve-hour mission, he carries cigars, cigarettes, loose tobacco, and a pipe. Should his plane be shot down, Tibbets also has a handgun. And, should capture become a possibility, he also carries twelve cyanide pills, one for each member of his crew. Better to end their lives than be tortured into giving away A-bomb secrets.

Tibbets knew there would be commotion about tonight's mission. But he never expected the sight before him: Floodlights turn the black tropical night into day. Flashbulbs pop as Tibbets and his crew arrive at the flight line. Scientists and technicians flit around the bomber, fussing over last-minute details. Inside the forward bomb bay, safely concealed from view, is the bulbous, 9,700-pound Little Boy, soon to be dropped from a height of five miles onto Hiroshima. The target point is the concrete-and-steel Aioi Bridge, its T shape easily visible from the air.

"There stood the *Enola Gay*," Tibbets will later write, "bathed in floodlights like the star of a Hollywood movie. Motion picture cameras were set up and still photographers were standing by with their equipment. Any Japanese lurking in the surrounding hills— and there were still some who had escaped capture—had to know that something very special was going on."

Soon, the thrum of the 2,200 horsepower B-29 engines fills the air as the advance weather planes *Jabit III*, *Full House*, and *Straight Flush* lumber down the 8,500-foot east-west Runway Able, which has been nicknamed the Hirohito Highway. One by one, the planes take off and ascend into the night for the twelve-hour round-trip flight to the Empire.

The time is 1:37 A.M.

Colonel Tibbets makes one last walk around *Enola Gay*, looking closely for signs of trouble. With seven thousand gallons of fuel and an almost five-ton bomb, she is nearly seven tons overweight, so even the slightest malfunction could be deadly.

"I made sure there were no open pieces of cowling, no pitot covers left hanging, and that the tires were inflated and in good condition. I also checked the pavement for telltale evidence of hydraulic leaks and looked into the bottom of the engine cowlings with a flashlight to be sure there was no excessive oil drip."

At 2:20 A.M., the crew photograph is taken. Then Tibbets enters the cockpit through a ladder at the front end of the nose gear. The other eleven members of the crew also get on the plane, find their seats, and arrange themselves for the long flight.

Tibbets sits in the seat on the left reserved for the aircraft commander. Captain Bob Lewis takes the copilot seat. There is tension between the two men, for *Enola Gay* was Lewis's aircraft before Tibbets chose to change the name and fly it on this mission. Outside, spectators wait patiently on the tarmac for *Enola Gay* to take flight. Tibbets is in no hurry, unworried about his audience or the bruised feelings of Captain Lewis as he runs through yet another preflight check of instruments and systems.

At 2:27 A.M. *Enola Gay*'s engines are started. Once all four engines are running, Tibbets does a final check of the oil pressure, fuel pressure, and RPMs. The thrum of the propellers causes *Enola Gay* to shake; only when she takes flight will the vibration cease. "The entire checkout and starting procedure required about thirty-five minutes, and it was now 2:30," Tibbets will remember.

"Waving to the crowd of almost one hundred well-wishers who were standing by, I gunned the engines and began our taxi. . . .

"Destination: Hiroshima."

CHAPTER 33

HIROSHIMA, JAPAN

August 6, 1945 • 7:10 A.M.

THE HUMID AIR is filled with warning. Air-raid sirens again awaken the citizens of Hiroshima. The morning has dawned warm and clear, with just a few wispy clouds in the sky. A single American B-29 has been seen flying toward the city, causing the alert to sound and disrupting the start of the business day—a time for cooking the morning meal and boarding the streetcar to work. Air-raid warnings are now a constant nuisance, but at this late point in the war it seems unlikely the Americans will finally bomb the city. So while some residents dutifully flee into bomb shelters, others go about their day.

In the huge harbor, shrimp fishermen tend to their nets, as their ancestors have done for centuries. They ignore the air-raid warnings, as they have nowhere to go. In the southern section of town near the port, the Ujina fire station is relatively calm, and fireman Yosaku Mikami looks at the clock. He is less than sixty minutes away from the end of his twenty-four-hour shift, but any bombing will cause fires, meaning Yosaku's services will be needed immediately.

Despite the evacuation of his family yesterday and the empty house that awaits him, Yosaku is eager to get home. He patiently waits for the sound of the all-clear siren, and at 7:31 A.M. he hears it. The danger has passed—or so it seems.

A B-25 takes off from the deck of an aircraft carrier. [National Archives]

CHAPTER 34

OVER THE PACIFIC

August 6, 1945 • 7:24 A.M.

ENOLA GAY FLIES TOWARD Japan at an altitude of 31,000 feet. Weather plane *Straight Flush*, which caused the air-raid sirens to sound in Hiroshima this morning, has just reported that the weather is fine for visual bombing. With that message, the fate of the city is sealed.

"It's Hiroshima," Colonel Paul Tibbets barks into *Enola Gay's* intercom.

Shortly after taking off from Tinian, Captain Deak Parsons and his assistant, Lieutenant Morris Jeppson, wriggled through the small pressurized opening separating the bomb bay from the rest of the aircraft. Little Boy almost entirely filled the cavernous space.

A single shackle held Little Boy in place. Braces kept the bomb from swaying side to side. Standing on a small catwalk, Parsons positioned himself at the rear of the device, and Jeppson, a physicist educated at Harvard, Yale, and MIT, provided some light.

The captain worked quickly, running through an eleven-step checklist that armed Little Boy. Opening a small panel, he inserted four silk packages of cordite powder. This smokeless propellant will detonate the uranium "bullet" at one end of the bomb's inner cannon barrel. The small chunk of enriched U-235 uranium will race down the barrel and collide with a separate sphere of uranium known as the nucleus at the opposite end. Within one-trillionth of a second of the bullet striking the nucleus—a picosecond, in technical terms—the splitting of one atom into two smaller atoms will begin the process of nuclear fission. The explosion will follow immediately, releasing deadly heat and radioactive gamma rays.

As Parsons worked, the sharp, machined edges of the rear panel cut his fingertips. Undaunted, he finished the job in twenty-five minutes. His final act was to insert three green dummy plugs between Little Boy's battery and its firing mechanism.

Little Boy is armed, but fragile. Anything that ignites the cordite charges will cause it to explode, killing all the men on *Enola Gay*; thus, the green plugs placed between the electrical connections. As long as those plugs are secure, Little Boy will not detonate.

About an hour ago, Parsons sent Jeppson back into the bomb bay one last time. The blond lieutenant replaced the green plugs with three red arming plugs, thus establishing an electrical circuit between the battery and the bomb.

Little Boy is alive.

CHAPTER 35

OVER HIRSOHIMA, JAPAN

August 6, 1945 • 8:14 A.M.

ENOLA GAY BOMBARDIER Major Thomas Ferebee is now in control of the plane. He announces, pointing straight out the front bubble window of the aircraft, "I've got the bridge."

The Aioi Bridge was chosen as Little Boy's aiming point because of its location in the center of Hiroshima and its unique T shape, visible from the air.

Looking down, Colonel Tibbets can see the white buildings of downtown Hiroshima; he can actually see a mass of movement that looks like people walking to work. "My eyes were fixed on the center of the city, which shimmered in the early morning light," he will later remember.

Enola Gay flies the last miles to Hiroshima uncontested. No enemy planes or antiaircraft fire greet the Americans. Japanese air defense officials, having already sounded three air-raid warnings during the night, choose to ignore the B-29s' approach, thinking it to be a simple reconnaissance mission.

With ninety seconds to go, Ferebee positions his left eye over the Norden bombsight's viewfinder. If he does his job properly, allowing for *Enola Gay*'s airspeed of 330 miles per hour and the slight amount of wind that will cause the bomb to drift, Little Boy should fall with pinpoint accuracy.

"One minute out," Tibbets announces.

Ferebee flicks a switch that sends a sharp tone into the headphones of the *Enola Gay* crew and those of the men in the two scientific planes, reminding them of what is to come. They are to put specially darkened goggles over their eyes to protect their vision. All three planes have been ordered to flee the vicinity as soon as possible to avoid the aftershock of the atomic explosion.

"Thirty seconds," says Tibbets.

"Twenty."

The bomb bay doors open at precisely 8:15 A.M.

"Ten . . . nine . . . eight . . . seven . . . six . . . five . . .

"Four . . . three . . . two . . . one . . ."

At 8:15:17 A.M., Little Boy is set loose from its shackle.

• • •

Instantly, *Enola Gay* lurches upward, finally rid of the extra tons behind its nose. Tibbets wrestles it sharply to the right, almost standing it on a wing as he turns away from Hiroshima. He has less than fifty seconds to distance himself from the blast. If he fails to cover enough ground, *Enola Gay* will be destroyed by shock waves.

Despite the sixty-degree bank, a move more suited to a lithe fighter aircraft than a massive bomber, bombardier Ferebee keeps his left eye affixed to his Norden bombsight, allowing him to watch Little Boy plummet to earth. The bomb wobbles after first being dropped, but the four stabilizing fins soon force the nose down, propelling it toward the heart of Hiroshima.

Ferebee is transfixed, knowing that he is witnessing history. Ten seconds pass. Twenty. Thirty. Almost too late, he remembers that the explosion's brightness will blind anyone who stares at it. Just in time, Ferebee unglues his eye from the bombsight and turns away from Little Boy's descent.

Notes of Robert Lewis on the bombing of Hiroshima.
[National Archives]

CHAPTER 36

HIROSHIMA, JAPAN

August 6, 1945 • 8:16 A.M.

ORTY-THREE SECONDS AFTER its release, at an altitude of
1,968 feet over the Aioi Bridge in downtown Hiroshima,
Little Boy's radar proximity fuse detonates. Within the bomb's
inner cannon, the four cordite charges explode, sending the uranium bullet hurtling the length of the barrel, where it collides with
the second mass of U-235. The chain reaction is instantaneous. In
the blast that follows, a fireball spreads out over the target zone. It
travels at one hundred times the speed of sound, rendering it silent.
One millionth of a second later, the people of Hiroshima begin to
incinerate.

Almost twelve miles away, the shock wave slams into the escap-
ing *Enola Gay* so hard that Tibbets shouts "Flak," thinking the plane
has been hit by ground fire. He feels a strange "tingling sensation"

in his mouth, the result of his fillings interacting with the radioactive elements now billowing thousands of feet into the air.

But *Enola Gay* is safe. All twelve men on board are alive. In six hours they will celebrate with whiskey and lemonade and spend the night far from the hell they have just created.

● ● ●

Little Boy explodes three hundred yards from its primary target. The temperature inside the bomb at the moment of nuclear fission is more than a million degrees Fahrenheit, which sends out a white flash of light ten times the brightness of the sun. As the surrounding air ignites, the sky erupts into a fireball three hundred yards wide. Millionths of a second later, the heat on the ground directly below spikes to 6,000 degrees.

Thousands of men, women, and children within a half-mile radius beneath the bomb's explosion are instantly reduced to lumps of charcoal, their internal organs evaporating inside their charred corpses. Downtown Hiroshima is littered in smoking black piles that were once human bodies.

But that is just the beginning.

Then comes the shock wave as the blast rockets outward with the force of sixteen thousand tons of TNT, followed immediately by a billowing mushroom cloud that rises more than fifty thousand feet into the air, sucking up dust and debris along with the vaporized remains of those killed beneath it.

Within seconds, seventy thousand people are dead.

Just after the bomb detonates, smoke billows 20,000 feet above Hiroshima and spreads more than 10,000 feet at the base. The photo was taken from the escort plane. [National Archives]

Almost every person and building within a one-mile radius of the explosion has vanished.

Pets, birds, rats, ants, cockroaches—gone.

Homes, fishing boats, telephone poles, the centuries-old Hiroshima Castle—all disappear.

Day turns into night as the mushroom cloud blots out the sun. Beyond the one-mile radius of the bomb's explosion, some have survived, though at a horrible cost. Flash burns maim and disfigure thousands, many of whom live miles away.

No one is spared the suffering. A group of students from the Hiroshima Girls Business School are "covered with blisters the size of balls, on their backs, their faces, their shoulders and their arms. The blisters were starting to burst open and their skin hung down like rugs," Japanese photojournalist Yoshito Matsushige will remember.

● ● ●

If the designers of Little Boy imagined a single bomb blast would inflict instant death on thousands, they were correct. The truth is that it does not take much imagination to foresee puncture wounds caused by shards of exploded glass and wood hurtling through the air. The atomic blast wave travels at two miles per second, knocking flat anything in its path. Then there is the horror of radiation—radioactive particles of dust that will slowly kill residents of Hiroshima for months and years to come. But there is even more.

Thousands of Japanese die from fire and water. The flames

[TOP AND BOTTOM] The destruction of Hiroshima. [National Archives]

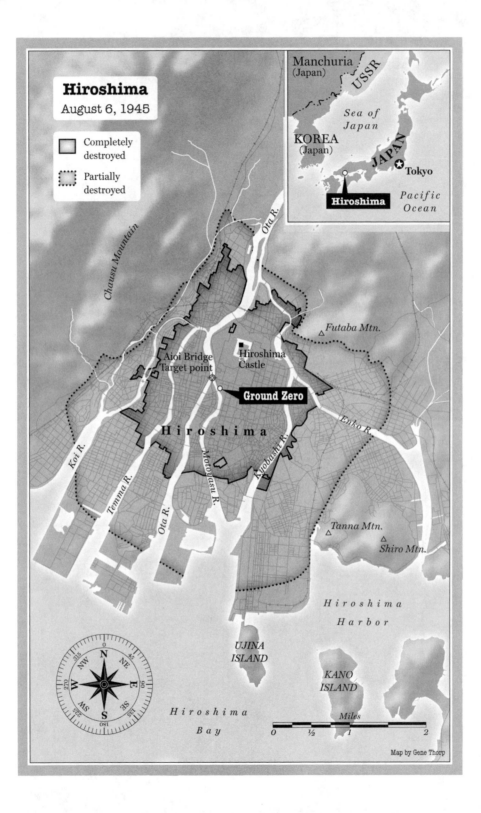

Hiroshima
August 6, 1945

Completely destroyed

Partially destroyed

Manchuria
(Japan)

USSR

Sea of
Japan

KOREA
(Japan)

JAPAN

Tokyo

Hiroshima

Pacific
Ocean

Chausu Mountain

Ota R.

Futaba Mtn.

Aioi Bridge
Target point

Hiroshima
Castle

Ground Zero

Enko R.

H i r o s h i m a

Koi R.

Temma R.

Motoyasu R.

Kyobashi R.

Ota R.

Tanna Mtn.

Shiro Mtn.

*Hiroshima
Harbor*

N
NW
NE
W
E
SW
SE
S

UJINA
ISLAND

KANO
ISLAND

*Hiroshima
Bay*

Miles

0   ½   1   2

Map by Gene Thorp

come first, individual blazes that begin the instant Little Boy explodes. Within five minutes, almost every structure within a two-mile radius of the blast is alight in a raging firestorm that propels a powerful flaming wind. Soon, that wind reaches hurricane strength, reducing much of Hiroshima to cinders.

Many residents are now buried in the rubble of their collapsed homes. Trapped beneath thick wooden beams and tons of ceramic roof tiling, they frantically plead for rescue as the fires burn closer. Their screams echo throughout the streets of Hiroshima.

To escape the firestorm, or to cool the burns covering their bodies, many Japanese leap into the city's firefighting cisterns. But what happens next is yet another cruel twist of fate: the explosion has superheated the water, and everyone immersing himself or herself in it immediately boils to death.

Others try to escape the flames by diving into one of the seven rivers that flow through Hiroshima, only to find the water clogged with dead bodies.

Hiroshima is chaos. Some confused citizens maintain almost total silence as they endure the horrors of Little Boy. Many wander the streets in a daze, arms held away from their bodies to prevent them from rubbing against their burns, staring at the carbon lumps on the street, picking their way through the debris, and absorbing the surreal nature of what has happened. Others, their homes destroyed, join the long line of Hiroshima's citizens frantically retreating to the safety of the countryside.

[FOLLOWING PAGES] The next three photographs show the charred remains of Hiroshima. [National Archives]

Part Three

Unconditional Surrender

CHAPTER 37

TOKYO, JAPAN

August 6, 1945 • 8:17 A.M.

J UST SECONDS AFTER LITTLE BOY'S detonation, the Japan Broadcasting Corporation in Tokyo notices that its Hiroshima station is off the air. The control operator gets on the phone to see if he can help fix the problem but gets no response.

Soon it becomes clear that Hiroshima's train station, telegraph operators, and military garrison have also severed communications. Fearing an American bombing, staff at the Japanese military headquarters in Tokyo dispatch a young officer to investigate. His orders are to fly to Hiroshima immediately and ascertain whether or not the city has been the target of an American attack.

Two days later, the chilling results of what the young officer saw from the air are reported on Tokyo English-language radio: "Practically all living things, human and animal, were literally seared to death."

CHAPTER 38

USS *AUGUSTA* ATLANTIC OCEAN

August 6, 1945 • Noon

HARRY TRUMAN IS FEELING powerful. Holding court just before lunch in the USS *Augusta*'s enlisted men's mess hall, he banters with the six sailors at his table, asking about their hometowns and life in the navy. Truman could have flown home after his three-week stay at the Potsdam conference in Germany, but his security agents recommended making the five-day transatlantic journey by sea because they feared an attack in the sky.

The voyage has been blustery, the windblown Atlantic covered in whitecaps and rolling swells. Yet Truman has risen early each morning for a walk on deck in the open air. The crew have been surprised to see the president wearing a broad smile during these

*President Truman works at his desk aboard the
USS* Augusta *during his return trip to the United States
after the Potsdam conference.* [National Archives]

morning constitutionals, despite the ongoing conflict in the Pacific. They cannot possibly know the tremendous feeling of success he feels after holding his own on the world stage at Potsdam, and even more important, they do not know that Truman is awaiting confirmation that an atomic bomb has been dropped on Japan.

The president has had a hard time keeping this top secret news to himself. There are a handful of journalists on board the ship, and on the day the *Augusta* set sail from Plymouth, England, Truman met with them to explain that America possessed the atomic bomb. He shared this staggering news safe in the knowledge that the media are forbidden from using the ship's radios and have no way of communicating the information. In this particular isolation, the talkative Truman gets to explain the A-bomb on his terms, and yet the weapon maintains its confidential status.

As Truman now chats with the young sailors prior to eating

lunch, Captain Frank H. Graham approaches the table holding a map of Japan and a teletype message. Hiroshima is circled in red pencil on the map. The message reads: "Hiroshima bombed visually. . . . Results clear cut successful in all respects. Visible effects greater than in any test. Conditions normal in airplane following delivery."

Truman's face lights up. "This is the greatest thing in history," he proclaims to Graham, enthusiastically shaking his hand. "It's time for us to get home."

The president then orders Graham to share the secret message with Secretary of State James F. Byrnes, sitting just a few tables away. A second teletype arrives moments later from Secretary of War Henry Stimson confirming the previous report. "Big bomb dropped on Hiroshima August 5 at 7:15 P.M. Washington time. First reports indicate complete success."

Truman can't help himself. Leaping to his feet, he taps his water glass with a fork. At first, there is confusion. These military men immediately rise to attention, realizing the impropriety of the president standing as they sit. But Truman waves them back down: "Please keep your seats and listen for a moment. I have an announcement to make. We have just dropped a new bomb on Japan which has more power than twenty thousand tons of TNT. It has been an overwhelming success!"

Bedlam sweeps through the mess hall. Cheers echo down the ship's passageways. A grinning Truman holds the teletype message aloft as he races from the mess hall and runs down the corridor to share the news with the *Augusta*'s officers. "We won the gamble," he shouts above the jubilant celebration.

Everyone believes that the end of the war has arrived.

They are wrong.

Within moments, dressed in a tan double-breasted suit and dark tie, President Truman films a message to the American people from his stateroom aboard the *Augusta*. He sits at a desk, a porthole visible over his right shoulder. The text of his speech was prepared long ago but only just released to the national media by the White House. But Truman's words, which are also being broadcast live on the radio, have a far more powerful effect than a print dispatch. For while this message may seem to be aimed at the American people, it is in fact a warning to the Japanese leadership.

"Sixteen hours ago an American plane dropped one bomb on Hiroshima and destroyed its usefulness to the enemy," he begins. Truman's tone is somber, but there is no doubt he feels justified in his decision. Even as he speaks, more leaflets are being dropped on Japan, encouraging the people to rise up and demand that their leaders surrender.

"The Japanese began the war from the air at Pearl Harbor. They have been repaid many fold. And the end is not yet. With this bomb we have now added a new and revolutionary increase in destruction to supplement the growing power of our armed forces. In their present form these bombs are now in production and even more powerful forms are in development.

"It is an atomic bomb. It is a harnessing of the basic power of the universe. The force from which the sun draws its power has been loosed against those who brought war to the Far East."

Truman then tells the history of the bomb's development, concluding with an unmistakable reminder that the job is not yet done. Only Japan's acceptance of the Potsdam Declaration and its terms of unconditional surrender will stop the bombings.

"We are now prepared to destroy more rapidly and completely every productive enterprise the Japanese have in any city. We shall destroy their docks, their factories, and their communications. Let there be no mistake: We shall completely destroy Japan's power to make war. . . . If they do not now accept our terms they may expect a rain of ruin from the air, the like of which has never been seen on earth."

Finally, Truman signs off. He does not need to order a second bomb to be dropped on Japan, for that command was given two weeks ago, on the same date he approved the Hiroshima attack. In fact, the order allows for bombings to continue as long there is a supply of atomic bombs.

The *Augusta* is just north of Bermuda as Truman completes his speech. The temperature is finally warming. Knowing that a media whirlwind awaits him upon his arrival home tomorrow, the president settles in to enjoy a day of sunshine, hoping for news of a Japanese surrender.

CHAPTER 39

IMPERIAL PALACE
TOKYO, JAPAN

August 6, 1945 • 7:50 P.M.

IT HAS BEEN ELEVEN HOURS and thirty-five minutes since Little Boy was dropped on Hiroshima. Many in the Japanese high command believe that the bomb was atomic, but the generals have withheld this news from their emperor all afternoon.

It is dusk, and Hirohito takes advantage of the warm August night to stroll the gardens of the Imperial Palace, completely unaware of what has happened in Hiroshima.

Suddenly, an aide from the Imperial Japanese Army approaches, which can only mean bad news. Such an intrusion on the emperor's solitude is unheard of except in a time of tragedy. In somber tones, the aide informs Hirohito that Hiroshima has been "attacked with

A Japanese soldier walks through destroyed Hiroshima.
[National Archives]

a special bomb from a U.S. bomber." The aide goes on to state that the Navy Ministry, which has been investigating the attack, believes that "most parts of the city" have ceased to exist.

The aide leaves, allowing Emperor Hirohito to ruminate on what he has just heard. Since the fall of Okinawa six weeks ago, he has known that Japan cannot win this war. For a reminder of the Americans' dominance, Hirohito need only look around the Imperial Palace: despite standing orders by the U.S. military that the emperor's palace should not be bombed, fires started by B-29 raids on Tokyo have leaped the great stone walls and moats surrounding his fortress and burned Hirohito's wooden residence to the ground. Hirohito and his family now live in the imperial library, adjacent to the enormous gardens in which the emperor now walks. All of the emperor's official business is conducted in a bunker sixty feet underground. In that way, he is similar to his deceased ally, the German leader Adolf Hitler.

Like Hitler, Hirohito has refused to surrender. He has persisted in the belief that the Soviets will help him negotiate peace with America. The emperor still believes that now. However, he is staggered by the news from Hiroshima.

If the reports from the city are true, Hirohito knows that only unconditional surrender will save Japan from complete destruction. This will mean the end of the twenty-five-hundred-year imperial dynasty—and perhaps the end of Hirohito's own life, should he be tried and found guilty of war crimes.

But five hours later, when President Harry Truman once again demands unconditional surrender from Japan, Hirohito's response will be utter silence.

While his devastated people suffer and die, the god-man continues his stroll.

CHAPTER 40

MANILA, PHILIPPINES

August 7, 1945 • 12:01 A.M.

ENERAL DOUGLAS MACARTHUR is appalled. It is just after midnight on Tuesday when an aide awakens him with news of the Hiroshima bombing. The general is hypersensitive to slights both perceived and real, and when it comes to the atomic bomb, there have been many. For the past three years, MacArthur has waged war on his terms, attacking when and where he wants. He knows the Japanese culture from his decades living in the Pacific and is confident they are on the verge of surrender.

Even though MacArthur wears the five-star rank of general of the army, President Truman has rarely consulted him about the state of the Pacific conflict—unlike George Marshall and Dwight Eisenhower, who routinely advise the president on matters of war. While Marshall has long known about the bomb and Eisenhower was made aware of it shortly after the Trinity explosion, MacArthur learned of its existence only one week ago.

MacArthur was never once asked about the A-bomb's tactical use in his theater of war. It is a situation, he believes, no different than if the A-bomb had been dropped on Europe without Eisenhower being informed.

MacArthur knows that would never happen.

Now, on top of those insults, comes the stunning realization that Harry Truman does not trust Douglas MacArthur.

On Sunday, August 5, the general received verbal confirmation that the bomb would be dropped the following day. However, this courtesy also contained a key element of misdirection: instead of Hiroshima, the courier from Washington informed the general that ground zero would be a lightly populated industrial district south of Tokyo.

Someone, somewhere, believes Douglas MacArthur cannot keep a secret.

Unfortunately, MacArthur's behavior lends credence to the view that he can't keep his mouth shut. On the morning of the Hiroshima explosion, still not knowing its true location or whether the mission had been a success, MacArthur called reporters to his office at Manila City Hall and, in off-the-record comments, coyly predicted, "The war may end sooner than we think."

The truth is that MacArthur approved of the industrial target. Showcasing the power of the explosion in an area almost completely devoid of civilians made military sense to him. The tragic slaughter

Portrait of General Douglas MacArthur with his signature corncob pipe and sunglasses.
[Mary Evans Picture Library]

of Manila's residents by the retreating Japanese just a few months ago is still fresh in MacArthur's memory; even before those senseless killings, the general had been openly opposed to targeting civilians.

At this point in his career, MacArthur's military training precludes him from publicly criticizing his commander in chief, but for the rest of his life he will privately share his views about August 6, 1945. "MacArthur once spoke eloquently to me about it," Richard Nixon will one day recount to reporters. (The future president served a year in the Pacific during World War II as a naval officer.) "He thought it a tragedy that the bomb was ever exploded. . . . MacArthur, you see, was a soldier. He believed in using force only against military targets, and that is why the nuclear thing turned him off."

MacArthur's personal pilot, Lieutenant Colonel Weldon "Dusty" Rhoades, will remember MacArthur's opinion of the bomb even more vividly, writing in his journal, "General MacArthur definitely is appalled and depressed by this Frankenstein monster."

Accurately, MacArthur believes that bombing Hiroshima will not lead to a Japanese surrender. The shame would be overwhelming.

According to MacArthur, a Japanese surrender will happen only if President Truman allows the emperor to remain in power after the war. "The retention of the institution of the emperor," he argues, would allow the Japanese nation to seek peace with dignity, knowing that their divine emperor will continue to guide them.

CHAPTER 41

UNITED STATES

August 7, 1945

BUT MOST AMERICANS SEE the situation far differently.

"Thank God for the atomic bomb" is a common refrain among American soldiers and sailors, who have been dreading the bloodbath sure to come if American troops invade the beaches of Japan. To many of them, the bombing of civilians is not an issue—it's payback for the Japanese attack on Pearl Harbor. And if the destruction could lead to peace, U.S. enlisted men almost unanimously believe it is worth it. For the first time since they put on that uniform, these soldiers and sailors can start planning for the distant future. "For all the fake manliness of our facades," a twenty-one-year-old infantry lieutenant will write, "we cried with relief and joy. We were going to live. We were going to grow up to adulthood."

Later, a Gallup poll will report that 85 percent of Americans believe that the use of the atomic bomb is justified. Most of the media also support the decision. Across the country, newspapers trumpet the A-bomb blast in banner headlines. The *New York Times* reports the event with six front-page stories.

The *Times*, however, sounds a rare cautionary note, predicting that the use of the A-bomb will now be justified by other nations in the future. "Yesterday man unleashed the atom to destroy man, and another chapter in human history opened, a chapter in which the weird, the strange, the horrible becomes the trite and the obvious. Yesterday we clinched victory in the Pacific, but we sowed the whirlwind."

The analytical piece was written by Hanson Baldwin, military editor of the *New York Times*. "Americans have become a synonym for destruction. And now we have been the first to introduce a new weapon of unknowable effects which may bring us victory quickly but will sow the seeds of hate more widely than ever."

There are others who display trepidation. After observing the explosion from aboard *The Great Artiste*, Manhattan Project physicist Luis Alvarez begins questioning the morality of using the bomb. In a letter to his son written on the return flight to Tinian, he ponders what he has just seen: "What regrets I have about being a party to killing and maiming thousands of Japanese civilians this morning are tempered with the hope that this terrible weapon we have created may bring the countries of the world together and prevent future wars."

David Lawrence, the conservative founder of the *United States News*, later to become *U.S. News & World Report*, will pen one of the most damning criticisms of Truman's decision: "We shall not soon purge ourselves of the feeling of guilt which prevails among us. Military necessity will be our constant cry in answer to criticism, but it will never erase from our minds the simple truth that we, of all civilized nations, though hesitating to use poison gas, did not hesitate to employ the most destructive weapon of all times indiscriminately against men, women and children. What a precedent for the future we have furnished to other nations even less concerned than we with scruples or ideals!"

CHAPTER 42

JAPAN

August 8, 1945

I N JAPAN, THERE IS simply shock, but no talk of accepting the Potsdam Declaration and surrendering. Instead, as a wave of sixty-nine B-29 bombers attacks Tokyo with conventional bombs, the military broadcasts a series of defiant radio messages from the capital. The people of Japan are directed to remain calm in the face of American bombings and to renew their pledge to continue the fight.

An August 8 broadcast in English, aimed at North America, accuses the United States of an "atrocity campaign" that will "create the impression that the Japanese are cruel people." And while Japan has ignored the terms of the Geneva and Hague Conventions throughout the war, it is the United States that the Japanese now accuse of war crimes. "This is made clear by Article 22 of the

Hague Convention. Consequently, any attack by such means against open towns and defenseless citizens are unforgivable actions."

The broadcast asks: "How will the United States war leaders justify their degradation, not only in the eyes of the other peoples but also in the eyes of the American people? How will these righteous-thinking American people feel about the way their war leaders are perpetuating this crime against man and God?

"Will they condone the whole thing on the ground that everything is fair in love and war or will they rise in anger and denounce this blot on the honor and tradition and prestige of the American people?"

In an unusual attempt to win the sympathy of Europeans, another broadcast is transmitted in French. "As a consequence of the use of the new bomb against the town of Hiroshima on August Sixth, most of the town has been completely destroyed and there are numerous dead and wounded among the population.

"The destructive power of these bombs is indescribable, and the cruel sight resulting from the attack is so impressive that one cannot distinguish between men and women killed by the fire. The corpses are too numerous to be counted.

"The destructive power of this new bomb spreads over a large area. People who were outdoors at the time of the explosion were burned alive by high temperatures while those who were indoors were crushed by falling buildings."

CHAPTER 43

SOVIET UNION

August 8, 1945

THE DICTATOR JOSEPH STALIN declares war on Japan and is set to invade Japanese-held territory in Manchuria. The plan for that sneak attack has been kept from Harry Truman and America, as Stalin has rightly assessed Japan's weakness.

The Soviet Union's invasion of Manchuria is the last epic battle of the Second World War. The clash occurs on a scale comparable to the Allied invasion of Normandy on June 6, 1944; 1.5 million Russian soldiers face off against 700,000 Japanese troops. The Soviets rout the Japanese within a matter of weeks, losing an estimated 12,000 men killed and 24,000 men wounded. Japanese casualties are 22,000 killed and another 20,000 wounded, but just as debilitating is a historical rarity: mass desertion in the ranks. As in so many Russian conquests throughout Europe, rape and looting in

Manchuria quickly follow. The joy many Chinese felt upon being liberated from their Japanese captors is soon replaced by fear and loathing for the Soviets.

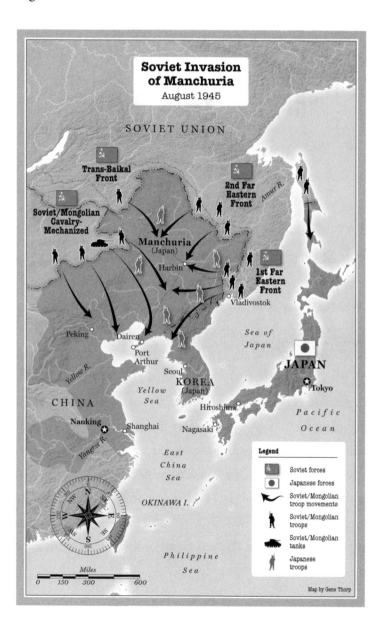

CHAPTER 44

MANILA, PHILIPPINES

August 9, 1945

I N HIS MANILA OFFICE, General Douglas MacArthur greets the news of the Manchurian invasion with great joy: "I am delighted at the Russian declaration of war against Japan. This will make possible a great pincer movement which cannot fail to end in the destruction of the enemy. In Europe, Russia was on the eastern front, with the Allies on the west. Now the Allies are on the east and the Russians on the west. But the result will be the same."

Like many other top American military leaders, MacArthur still sees Joseph Stalin as an ally, not an enemy. He has previously told other officers that "we must not invade Japan proper unless the Russian army is previously committed to action in Manchuria," believing that such an invasion would pin down Japanese divisions that might otherwise be shifted to fight against American forces.

The general also thinks that Soviet occupation of large segments of China and Korea is "inevitable"—not realizing he will one day be called upon to fight the communist advance in those areas.

It has now been three days since the atomic bomb was dropped. The Japanese have chosen not to surrender, and MacArthur is still hoping to lead the greatest amphibious invasion in the history of the world. To the general's way of thinking, another A-bomb is not needed.

America has *him*.

CHAPTER 45

IMPERIAL PALACE TOKYO, JAPAN

August 9, 1945 • 10:30 A.M.

EMPEROR HIROHITO IS MOROSE. He again walks through the elms and pine trees of his extensive garden, knowing the war is lost. He is brooding about the destruction of Hiroshima—he knows it has crushed the spirit of the Japanese people, and now there is even more horrible news: the Soviet Union has invaded Manchuria.

Although he is protected in a bunker, he understands his people are not. The United States has been bombing Japan for months, destroying so many cities that they are running out of targets. Tokyo itself has been hit more than a dozen times. Just yesterday, the emperor once again heard air-raid sirens throughout his capital city as sixty-nine B-29s bombed a nearby aircraft factory. The Japanese people are weary of war, but they continue to endure it, hoping to save their god-king from shame.

The invasion of Manchuria makes surrender inevitable. The Soviet Union and Japan signed a nonaggression pact four years ago, which Stalin has now violated. Hirohito knows the Russians to be an aggressive people. The Soviet entry into the Pacific war makes it possible that the Soviets may also attempt to invade mainland Japan. Hirohito's nation has neither the men nor the arms to hold off a two-pronged American and Soviet invasion.

Ignoring the heat, Hirohito continues to ponder the possibility of surrender. But this path is fraught with peril: the Japanese military might not cooperate. Some military and civilian leaders actually welcome the coming invasion for the chance to make a historic last stand against people they consider to be barbarians. If it comes to a final battle on Japanese soil, War Minister Korechika Anami believes, "we could at least for a time repulse the enemy, and might thereafter somehow find life out of death."

Even as the emperor absorbs the terrible news about the Soviet attack in Manchuria, the Supreme Council for the Direction of the War is meeting in the concrete bunker beneath the residence of Prime Minister Kantaro Suzuki to discuss whether to accept the Potsdam Declaration and take the first steps toward surrender.

Hirohito knows that surrender to the Americans will require the complete backing of his military. Despite Hirohito's divine imperial reign, it is the military that truly holds power in Japan.

It has been almost ten years, but Hirohito well remembers the terrible events of 1936, when an attempted military coup saw the assassination of several top government officials and the takeover of downtown Tokyo.

A faction loyal to Hirohito was successful in crushing the revolt, but there is no certainty the results will be the same should such a coup attempt happen again.

Despite the unprecedented carnage in Hiroshima, the god-man continues to dither.

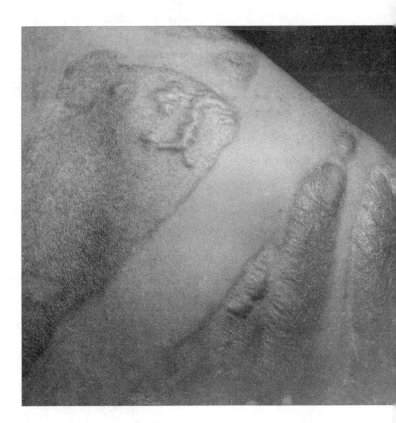

CHAPTER 46

HIROSHIMA, JAPAN

August 9, 1945

WITHIN DAYS, THE EXODUS FROM HIROSHIMA is complete. More than 150,000 residents travel by military truck or train to temporary shelters. The island of Ninoshima, five miles offshore in Hiroshima Bay and untouched by the A-bomb blast, is a storehouse for medical supplies and becomes the region's biggest relief center, providing comfort to more than ten thousand burn victims. The number of injured quickly overwhelms the available hospital beds, leading many of the burned and maimed to sleep in stables and other enclosures.

These scars were caused by the combination of burns from the heat of the bomb and poisoning from radioactive soot and dust that fell from the cloud.
[National Archives]

Bacterial infection of wounds exposed to the extreme smoke and debris of the blast runs rampant.

Compare this post-attack mosaic of Hiroshima with the pre-attack photograph on pages 108–109. [National Archives]

POST-ATTACK MOSAIC
(UNCONTROLLED)
HIROSHIMA
PHOTOS OF II AUGUST 1945

0   2000   4000
   1000   3000   5000
        FEET

PHOTO 2-II (PS)   SECRET

SECRET

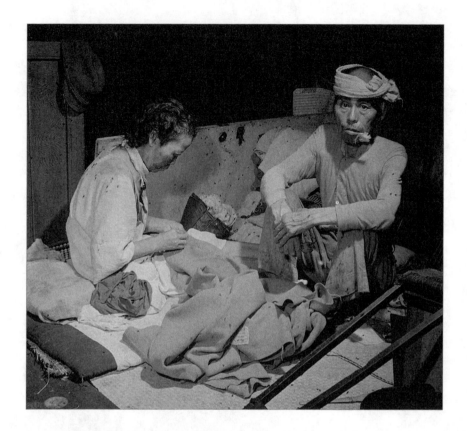

Victims of the bombing wait in a makeshift hospital in a bank building that survived the blast. [National Archives]

Teams of doctors perform surgery around the clock, seeing so many patients that there is no time to clean the operating theater between victims; the most common procedure is amputation.

Yet the amputees are the lucky ones. At least they are alive and can begin planning for a new future; many victims of the blast who come to Ninoshima seeking medical help die within days from their infections and burns. At first, their corpses are stacked one on top of the other for burning. But soon the number of dead bodies is so great that mass cremation becomes impossible. Instead, the dead are carried to air-raid shelters and former quarantine centers. These impromptu burial sites will be excavated decades later, uncovering not just bone fragments and ashes but artifacts like rings and buckles that will help reveal the identities of the dead.

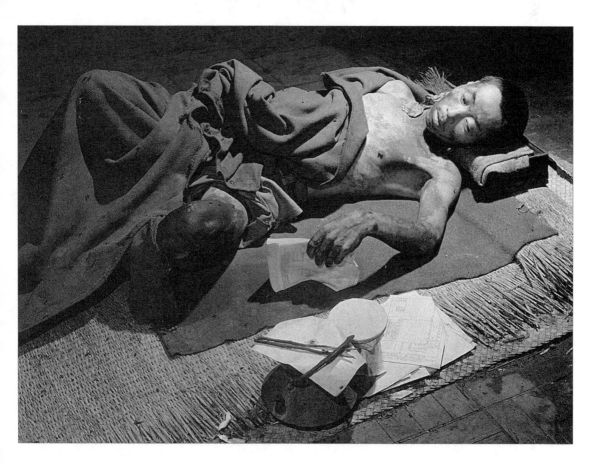

A burn patient awaits treatment. [National Archives]

CHAPTER 47

NORTH FIELD
TINIAN, MARIANA ISLANDS

August 9, 1945 • 3:47 A.M.

T HE NEXT RUN does not begin well.

The first issue is the weather. Monsoon conditions and a typhoon gathering strength around Iwo Jima mean the window for dropping the second A-bomb is closing fast. It is either go now or wait a week. The mission has been moved up.

Complications begin late in the evening of August 8, when nuclear engineers assembling Fat Man's firing unit almost detonate the device by inserting a cable into the assembly backward. The problem is fixed, but not before the two engineers spend several nervous minutes sweating fearfully as they switch and resolder the connectors, terrified all the while that Fat Man will blow them up.

The nose of Bockscar. *The art was painted on after the bombing mission.*
[Getty Images]

At midnight soldiers take Fat Man away and load it onto *Bockscar*. Before the crews board the planes, they receive last-minute changes to the plan. Because of the weather, they are to fly at higher than usual altitudes and rendezvous over Yakushima.

A further complication arises during the preflight check, when it is discovered that the fuel in *Bockscar*'s reserve tank is not pumping. This could become a problem because flying at higher altitudes burns more fuel. But the mission has to proceed.

And so *Bockscar* takes off at 3:47 A.M. on August 9, 1945. Like *Enola Gay*, it uses the entire length of Tinian's runway before pilot Major Charles Sweeney coaxes it up into the thick tropical air.

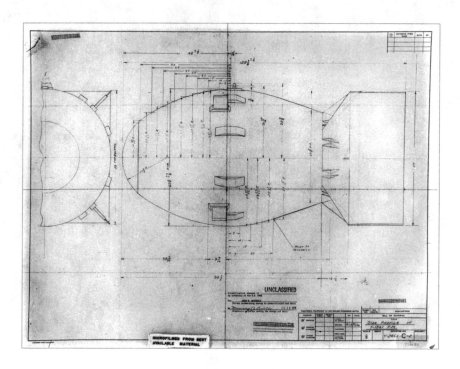

Diagram of Fat Man. [Los Alamos National Laboratory]

Already exhausted and wanting to be sharp later in the flight, Major Sweeney immediately hands the controls off to his copilot, Lieutenant Charles Donald Albury, so he can catch a few hours' sleep. The weather is volatile, a mixture of lightning, rain, and winds from the distant typhoon. *Bockscar* fights through the chop as it climbs to seventeen thousand feet.

At 4:00 A.M., Frederick Ashworth, the mission's chief weaponeer, replaces the bomb's green safety plugs with red.

Fat Man is armed.

Fat Man is placed on a trailer cradle outside the building where it was assembled.
[National Archives]

CHAPTER 48

TINIAN, MARIANA ISLANDS

August 9, 1945

COLONEL PAUL TIBBETS still has not seen the awful destruction that he and his men delivered to Hiroshima. Right now that is not his primary concern. There has been a report that *Bockscar*, the plane carrying the second A-bomb, is lost at sea. Whether this means it has crash-landed in the Pacific or the new plutonium bomb exploded en route to the target, Tibbets does not know. Fearing the worst, he can only hope that the ominous radio message "*Bockscar* down" was garbled in transmission.

Even though General Curtis LeMay wanted Tibbets to lead the second atomic bombing mission, the colonel chose to hand over the job to Chuck Sweeney, his close friend. Tibbets wanted Sweeney to have a chance to go down in history. The twenty-five-year-old Bostonian flew *The Great Artiste* in the Hiroshima mission, witnessing the giant mushroom cloud that rose over the city as his plane's scientific instruments measured radioactivity and blast force. Sweeney seemed an ideal choice to lead the second atomic bombing run over Japan, having served as a squadron commander for three months and flown five simulated A-bomb attack missions. Tibbets also knows him to be a rule follower, a man who will execute his orders precisely as they have been written.

The one flaw in Sweeney's résumé is that he has never before flown in combat.

• • •

Although Tibbets is unaware of it, *Bockscar* has a problem. The rendezvous with the instrument plane and the photographic plane was supposed to take place at thirty thousand feet around 9:00 A.M. Sweeney had specific orders from Colonel Tibbets to remain at the rendezvous point for no more than fifteen minutes. *The Great Artiste*, still outfitted with scientific instruments, showed up on time, but *Big Stink*, the photographic plane, was nowhere to be seen.

"Where's Hoppy?" Sweeney demanded, referring to the pilot of the missing B-29. "Where the hell is Hoppy?"

Defying Tibbets's order, Sweeney circled for forty-five long minutes, burning more and more fuel. He wanted this mission to be perfect, just like that of *Enola Gay*. He waited at the rendezvous until he could wait no more.

Finally, just before 10:00 A.M., Sweeney broke off and flew toward Kokura.

● ● ●

Major James I. "Hoppy" Hopkins and *Big Stink* were in fact in the area the entire time. But Hopkins was at an incorrect altitude, nine thousand feet above *Bockscar* and *The Great Artiste*.

Growing more concerned by the minute, Hopkins finally disobeyed orders and broke radio silence. "Is *Bockscar* down?" he asked the personnel back on Tinian.

The control tower heard only the words *"Bockscar* down"—leading to Colonel Tibbets's current angst and causing General Groves's deputy to step outside the mess hall and vomit up his breakfast. All ships and planes standing by for rescue operations are now told to stand down, as *Bockscar* is considered lost.

But nobody has told that to *Bockscar*'s crew. They are on their own.

● ● ●

Major Sweeney has not crashed, but he is experiencing visibility problems over Japan. The target is Kokura, a historic tree-lined city just 130 miles southwest of Hiroshima. It is one of Japan's most heavily defended cities, a hub of steelworks and munitions factories. Many Hiroshima residents who survived the first A-bomb blast have come here seeking refuge.

Sweeney's bomb bay doors are already open. The plutonium weapon known as Fat Man is ready for release. Yet Sweeney's orders forbid him from dropping Fat Man without a clear aerial view of

The crew of Bockscar. *The commander, Major Charles Sweeney, stands at far right.*
[Los Alamos National Laboratory]

the target. Thirty minutes ago the weather report said it was cloudy but visibility was still good. Yet thick clouds are now making it impossible to distinguish Kokura's buildings from the air. Smoke from the nearby industrial city of Yawata, which was firebombed last night, has drifted over the city, mingling with the low clouds.

Frustrated bombardier Captain Kermit Beahan presses his left eye to the Norden bombsight's viewfinder, straining to see the target. Today is his twenty-seventh birthday. Through the crosshairs, Beahan glimpses a few random buildings but cannot see the large weapons factory that is the aiming point for Fat Man.

"No drop!" he yells.

An increasingly frustrated Sweeney turns *Bockscar* in a steep bank. Determined to follow orders, he is taking a great risk by flying a second bombing run over the city, because there is now determined opposition. Japanese antiaircraft fire explodes all around him, proving to the surprised American crew that the enemy still possesses hidden defenses. Ashworth climbs into the cockpit to remind Sweeney that *Bockscar* has a fully armed A-bomb in its belly. It is behind schedule and running out of gas. Everything that can possibly go wrong on this mission has gone wrong.

"Major," says tail gunner Sergeant Albert "Pappy" Dehart over the intercom, "flak is closer."

"Roger," Sweeney answers, his voice flat and grim.

Dehart's voice comes over the intercom again, this time high and tight: "Flak right on our tail and coming closer."

"Skipper," radar operator Sergeant Edward K. Buckley breaks in, "Jap Zeros coming up at us. Looks like about ten."

And still bombardier Beahan cannot see a thing.

"Let's try it from another angle," Sweeney barks over the intercom, ignoring the news of approaching fighter planes as he lines up for a third run.

But when Beahan still cannot find the target, Sweeney and Ashworth discuss their options. Ashworth advocates turning to Nagasaki, and Sweeney turns the plane to the secondary target.

"Radar or visually," Ashworth says, "but drop we will."

Bockscar's bomb bay doors are immediately closed. The Japanese Zeros have not yet arrived, but Sweeney pushes *Bockscar* to the limit to escape.

The crew, which has grown fearful, cheers. "Nagasaki, here we come."

• • •

Grasping the steering wheel tightly, Sweeney banks southwest toward Nagasaki, ninety-five miles away. He turns so severely that *Bockscar* almost collides midair with *The Great Artiste*, which has been following them to record the power of the blast. Sweeney's jitters are compounded by the knowledge that his aircraft has only enough fuel for one bombing run if he hopes to land 450 miles away at Okinawa on his return. Even that is a stretch—he may have to crash-land *Bockscar* in the Pacific after dropping the bomb. The thought is weighing heavily on his mind.

• • •

Nagasaki is a town of some romance, first visited by Portuguese sailors in the sixteenth century and so beloved by European tourists that it became the setting for Italian composer Giacomo Puccini's opera *Madama Butterfly*. It is also a major port city for the Japanese

war effort and home to both the Mitsubishi Steel and Armament Works and the torpedo-producing Mitsubishi-Urakami Ordnance Works.

Sweeney levels off at twenty-eight thousand feet for the bombing run, but Nagasaki is just as covered by clouds as Kokura. Bombardier Beahan is prepared to violate orders and use radar to locate the target as Sweeney begins the five-minute bombing run over the city.

"I got it," an excited Beahan suddenly yells, seeing the unmistakable shape of a Nagasaki racetrack through a hole in the clouds. He immediately switches from radar to visual bombardment. *Bockscar*'s airspeed is just two hundred miles per hour.

Within forty-five seconds, Beahan spots the target and drops Fat Man.

"Bomb away," he announces. The black five-ton bomb tumbles out of the bay, destined to explode in forty-three seconds.

Immediately, Sweeney dives *Bockscar* down and banks to the right, racing away

A mushroom cloud rises over Nagasaki after the explosion of Fat Man. [National Archives]

from the coming mushroom cloud. *The Great Artiste* follows. The blast force far exceeds that of Little Boy. Five shock waves pound the two planes as they make their escape, a sensation that feels like "being beaten by a telegraph pole" to Sweeney. Within moments, both planes are out over the sea.

"Mayday, Mayday," Sweeney says, breaking radio silence. He is desperately trying to signal any American military craft in the area that *Bockscar* is in trouble—almost out of fuel. His radio call is heard back in Tinian, reassuring them that the mission has not been aborted and that the men of *Bockscar* are still alive. Yet there is little anyone but Sweeney can do to get *Bockscar* safely to Okinawa; all rescue operations were suspended when it was feared that *Bockscar* had crashed. The flight engineer, Master Sergeant John D. Kuharek, estimates that their three hundred remaining gallons of fuel will leave them fifty miles short.

For more than an hour, Sweeney and the men of *Bockscar* pray. They fly over open ocean, knowing all too well there is no margin for error. Each man dons his flotation device in case of a water landing. Sweeney slows the propellers to decrease fuel use and lowers his elevation a little at a time, allowing gravity to provide airspeed. Many of the men believe they will not make it. *Bockscar*'s navigator, Lieutenant Fred Olivi, wonders if the water will be cold.

Okinawa finally comes into view. In the short few weeks since the Allies conquered the island, its runways have become congested and busy; rows of bombers preparing for takeoff line the runway apron. Unable to raise the control tower on the radio, Sweeney orders that emergency flares be fired out the plane's upper porthole, hoping the runways will be cleared.

They are.

Bockscar lands at 1:51 P.M., traveling so fast that upon initial impact it bounces twenty-five feet into the air. One by one, the engines shut down for lack of fuel. Struggling to control his floundering aircraft, Sweeney just misses a row of B-24 bombers laden with incendiary bombs, which would have killed him and his crew in a massive fiery explosion.

Finally, *Bockscar* comes to a halt. Emergency fire trucks and ambulances race to its assistance. The bomber has hardly enough fuel to taxi off the runway. Incredibly, no one has informed the airfield that *Bockscar* was en route.

"Who the hell are you?" demands base commander Lieutenant General Jimmy Doolittle, the man whose daring raid on Tokyo in 1942 marked the first American attack on Japanese soil. It is a fitting moment: the first man to bomb Japan in the Second World War is squaring off with with the man who hopes to be the last.

"We are the 509, *Bockscar*," comes the reply. "We dropped an atomic bomb on Nagasaki."

CHAPTER 49

NAGASAKI, JAPAN

August 9, 1945

FAT MAN IS INDEED off target, missing the Mitsubishi torpedo plant by almost two miles.

On the ground, an estimated 45,000 men, women, and children die instantly; another 60,000 are badly injured. Although there are fires in the city, there is no firestorm, as in Hiroshima, because Fat Man detonates in the steep, wooded Urakami Valley. The uneven terrain prevents the blast from expanding far outward and blocks winds that would stoke the flames. However, the traumatic flash burns and the carbonization of the dead and dying are no less intense.

Once again, thousands are crushed in the rubble of their own homes and businesses. The unique construction of Nagasaki's bomb shelters, which are mostly caves dug into the hillsides, turns the stone passageways into ovens that burn hundreds alive in an instant. Throughout the city, many of the burned walk for miles before collapsing and dying. Thousands of victims watch their skin grow yellow; they are doomed to die weeks and months later from radiation poisoning. The city of Nagasaki, having no place to bury all the bodies, establishes open-air crematoriums to burn the dead.

Survivors evacuate Nagasaki after the bombing.
[National Archives]

The gate to a Shinto shrine still stands one-half mile from ground zero in Nagasaki,
August 10, 1945. [National Archives]

CHAPTER 50

THE WHITE HOUSE
WASHINGTON, D.C.

August 9, 1945 • 10:46 A.M.

A VICIOUS WAVE OF HEAT and humidity envelops the nation's capital. President Truman has received news of the successful Nagasaki mission.

Truman does not wish to obliterate the Japanese; he wants them to surrender. Early reports show heavy civilian casualties in Nagasaki, just as in Hiroshima. Yet the Japanese military seems willing to endure such horrific losses.

"For myself, I certainly regret the necessity of wiping out whole populations because of the 'pigheadedness' of the leaders of a nation," Truman will write to Senator Richard Russell, a Democrat from Georgia. "My object is to save as many American lives as possible but I also have a humane feeling for the women and children in Japan."

Truman is expressing his sympathy, not reversing his position. He is as adamant as ever that he will do what it takes to defeat the Japanese.

The president makes this abundantly clear to Samuel McCrea Cavert of the Federal Council of Churches of Christ in America, who has demanded that the president justify the dropping of atomic bombs.

A telegram from Cavert to the president reads, "Their use sets extremely dangerous precedent for future of mankind." The cable goes on to urge that "ample opportunity be given Japan to reconsider her ultimatum before any further devastation by atomic bomb is visited upon her people."

Cavert's message angers Truman. He will not be cowed. Normally he would not respond, particularly at a time when he is immersed in the high-stakes decisions of war, but this is not a time for silence. Truman dictates a direct response.

"Nobody is more disturbed over the use of Atomic bombs than I am but I was greatly disturbed over the unwarranted attack by the Japanese on Pearl Harbor and the murder of our prisoners of war," Truman says. "The only language they seem to understand is the one we have been using to bombard them.

"When you have to deal with a beast you have to treat him as a beast. It is most regrettable but nevertheless true."

CHAPTER 51

TOKYO, JAPAN

August 10, 1945 • 2:00 A.M.

THE LEADER OF THE BEAST, Emperor Hirohito, rises to speak in his underground bunker. He wears a full-dress military uniform. The weariness of yet another day and night of ruination is etched upon his face. Witnesses to this moment will remember the emperor being disheveled, his face flushed, his hair unkempt.

The emperor has hosted the Supreme Council for the Direction of the War and their assorted secretaries and assistants in the underground conference room for almost three hours. The thick wooden door is closed, and the ventilation is not working, causing every man to sweat from the extreme humidity in the chamber that is no bigger than a large bedroom. Even the lacquered wall panels bead with condensation.

The subject of this midnight meeting is unconditional surrender. It is the continuation of a long day of high-level war discussions, following close on the heels of the Soviet invasion and the Nagasaki bombing. Every man is exhausted. Each individual in this room has a personal stake in the discussion. Not only would surrender mean the end of the Japanese empire, but two days ago in England the Allies formalized an agreement stipulating the proper punishment of war criminals. The first men to be tried will be the Nazis; their trials will convene in the German city of Nuremberg starting this November.

If they surrender, the men in this overheated room will be next—and they know it.

All associated with the war realize they will most likely be tried and found guilty, even the emperor. Current Prime Minister Kantaro Suzuki, War Minister Korechika Anami, Navy Minister Mitsumasa Yonai, Foreign Minister Shigenori Togo, Chief of the Navy General Staff Soemu Toyoda, and Chief of the Army General Staff Yoshijiro Umezu recognize that whether they committed atrocities or not doesn't matter—they directed the soldiers and sailors who did.

Of course, Hirohito was the ultimate authority.

●　●　●

Particularly responsible is the man viewed worldwide as the Hitler of Japan, Hideki Tojo, the architect of the Japanese war effort who served as prime minister from October 1941 until July 1944.

It was the unassuming but manipulative Tojo who convinced Hirohito that war was necessary "to establish a new, stable order in East Asia." Tojo oversaw the surprise attacks throughout the Pacific that began this brutal war—a conflict that has now claimed twenty-four million lives in the Pacific and Asia alone. And it was Tojo who not only started the war but also authorized the inhumane policies

Emperor Hirohito (center), at a military review in Tokyo, has just handed a message to his war minister, Lieutenant General Hideki Tojo, October 21, 1941. [National Archives]

that will define the Japanese war effort far longer than any moment of strategic brilliance.

But he is not here for this imperial conference, and the men in this bunker allowed it all to happen.

● ● ●

Hirohito is at last ready to offer his opinion to the Supreme Council. Every man in the room rises and bows to his ruler. As they take their seats, the emperor is momentarily overcome by what he is about to say. But he gathers himself and proceeds. "Thinking about the world situation and the internal Japanese situation . . . to continue the war now means that cruelty and bloodshed will still continue in the world and that the Japanese nation will suffer severe damage."

The emperor's voice is high. He speaks quietly, in clipped sentences. As Hirohito's emotions get the best of him, he begins to cry. Many in the room are also overcome; they hurl themselves forward onto their conference tables and begin to sob.

Hirohito continues: "When I think about my obedient soldiers abroad, and of those who died or were wounded in battle, about those who have lost their property or lives by bombing in the homeland—when I think of all those sacrifices I cannot help but feel sad.

"I cannot stand the disarming of loyal and gallant troops and punishment of those responsible for war. . . .

"It is now necessary to bear the unbearable."

CHAPTER 52

THE WHITE HOUSE WASHINGTON, D.C.

August 10, 1945 • 6:30 A.M.

PRESIDENT TRUMAN RECEIVES the Japanese surrender letter in his private quarters at the White House. In the absence of a Japanese embassy in Washington, which has not existed since the attack on Pearl Harbor, Hirohito has sent the communiqué to the embassy of neutral Switzerland, which then passed it on to the War Department.

"In obedience to the gracious command of His Majesty the Emperor," the document begins, "the Japanese Government are ready to accept the terms enumerated in the joint declaration which was issued at Potsdam on July 26th, 1945, by the heads of the

Governments of the United States, Great Britain, and China, and later subscribed to by the Soviet Government."

Thus far, there is nothing in the language to deflate Truman's hopes for an unconditional surrender. This unlikely man who was nominated for the vice presidency just one year ago and who assumed the mantle of president of the United States at a most pivotal moment in world history is just a few sentences away from ending the Second World War. The German surrender in May was inevitable; the Japanese situation has been much trickier and has required Truman to show diplomatic steel to match America's military might. He has made many difficult decisions, with poise and focus. The slip of paper he holds in his hand is the culmination of four agonizing months in office. Yet he reads with trepidation, hoping the document is in accord with the surrender terms put forth by the United States.

It is not. The Japanese are attaching one vital condition to their surrender: "with the understanding that the said declaration does not comprise any demand which prejudices the prerogatives of His Majesty as a Sovereign Ruler."

Truman has been expecting this, and a small part of him may be willing to let Hirohito stay on the throne. Secretary of War Stimson has long argued that this is necessary to restore order in a postwar Japan. Certainly, General Douglas MacArthur has also made his conviction on this subject known.

But Truman is unsure: "Could we even consider a message with so large a 'but' as the kind of unconditional surrender we had fought for?" he will later write. It is a question that weighs heavily upon him.

The president is due to meet with his cabinet at 2:00 P.M. this Friday, but he hastily convenes a more discreet meeting to discuss the Japanese terms. In attendance are Stimson, Secretary of State James Byrnes, Secretary of the Navy James Forrestal, and Admiral William Leahy, Truman's chief of staff.

The room splits. Byrnes favors pushing for unconditional surrender; Stimson still maintains that the emperor is vital to Japan's postwar rehabilitation. Truman, who has already decided that no further atomic bombs will be dropped without his specific orders,

President Truman (fourth from right) meets with his cabinet to discuss terms of the Japanese surrender, August 10, 1945. [Harry S. Truman Library]

listens patiently to both sides. It is Forrestal who suggests there might be a loophole in the Potsdam terms that would allow the acceptance of Japan's surrender offer.

So it is that Truman orders that Japan be sent a counteroffer: Hirohito can remain, but he will not have immunity from war crimes.

"Ate lunch at my desk and discussed the Jap offer to surrender," Truman writes in his journal that night. "They wanted to make a condition precedent to the surrender. Our terms are 'unconditional.' They wanted to keep the Emperor. We told 'em we'd tell 'em how to keep him, but we'd make the terms."

The message is cabled to Switzerland, then on to Tokyo.

It reads: "With regard to the Japanese Government's message accepting the terms of the Potsdam proclamation but containing the statement, 'with the understanding that the said declaration does not comprise any demand which prejudices the prerogatives of His Majesty as a sovereign ruler,' our position is as follows:

"From the moment of surrender the authority of the Emperor and the Japanese Government to rule the state shall be subject to the Supreme Commander of the Allied powers who will take such steps as he deems proper to effectuate the surrender terms."

One day passes without word from the Japanese. Then another.

And still another.

Truman seethes.

CHAPTER 53

THE WHITE HOUSE WASHINGTON, D.C.

August 13, 1945 • 9:00 A.M.

THE PRESIDENT IS AT WORK in the Oval Office. Sensing that the Japanese will not accept his counteroffer, he authorizes the resumption of B-29 bombing raids utilizing conventional and incendiary bombs. Truman spends the afternoon with Lieutenant General Richard Sutherland, chief of staff for General Douglas MacArthur. The topic of discussion is the upcoming invasion of Japan. But there is another item Truman wishes to discuss with the fifty-one-year-old Sutherland, having to do with a secret plan the president has concocted to have Douglas MacArthur oversee the postwar rebuilding of Japan.

Meanwhile, as they have for almost a week, exhausted reporters and photographers crowd into the White House press briefing room, awaiting surrender news.

Outside, on the streets of Washington, rumors of an impending surrender are the talk of the day. In Lafayette Square, just across the street from the White House, citizens hold a vigil, longing to be at the epicenter of events when news of the Japanese capitulation is finally announced.

And still, there is nothing but silence from Japan.

Tuesday, August 14, is more of the same.

August is normally a time when the government goes on holiday to avoid the heat of Washington, but Truman obviously cannot leave.

Truman's outward behavior is calm. Reporters comment on his "cool stride" and "matter-of-factness."

Outside the White House, the crowd in Lafayette Square has now swelled to ten thousand. The press is still on round-the-clock standby, afraid of leaving the White House for even an instant.

Cameramen and sound technicians wait at the White House for news that Japan has surrendered, August 14, 1945.
[Harry S. Truman Library]

CHAPTER 54

TOKYO, JAPAN

August 14, 1945

I N TOKYO, HUNDREDS of thousands of leaflets fell into the streets two days ago, dropped by American B-29 bombers. They told the Japanese people that resistance was no longer realistic.

Now, prompted by the ongoing silence of the Japanese leadership, another massive flight of more than eight hundred B-29s thunders unopposed over Japan—only this time, their payload is not paper. In an act of redundancy, the Twentieth Air Force bombs what has already been bombed and obliterates what has already been obliterated in a massive show of force that is immediately nicknamed the Big Finale.

By 1:00 P.M. on the afternoon of Tuesday, August 14, as the people of Washington wait eagerly for the war's end, Japan blazes once more.

● ● ●

Emperor Hirohito does not see the flames. He remains in his quarters while outside his palace, rebellious junior officers of the Imperial Japanese Army are revolting. Their aim is to prevent the surrender of Japan by overthrowing Hirohito. But it is already too late.

Hirohito's agreement to the American terms of surrender has been transmitted to the neutral governments of Sweden and Switzerland. They were instructed to forward news of the acceptance to the leaders of the United States, Great Britain, China, and the Soviet Union. Then, in an act unparalleled in the history of Japan, the emperor met with technicians from NHK, the Japan Broadcasting Corporation, who recorded him reading the letter of surrender. Two phonographic records of this speech are now hidden within his wife's personal safe in the Imperial Palace.

The treasonous junior officers are led by Major Kenji Hatanaka. He and Captain Shigetaro Uehara have shot dead Lieutenant General Takeshi Mori, the commander of the Imperial Guards, for his refusal to join the revolt.

Utilizing Mori's personal stamp, rebellious officers create a false set of orders to fool seven Imperial Guard regiments, whose job it is to protect the emperor. The forged orders instruct a thousand troops to occupy the palace, seize all gates, and cut telephone lines. Soon, all communications between the Imperial Palace and the outside world are severed. Now Hatanaka and his allies begin searching the palace for two precious targets: the emperor himself and the recordings of his surrender speech. The Imperial Palace and its gardens sprawl across a swath of central Tokyo a mile wide; there are countless places the emperor could be hiding. Hatanaka and the soldiers are relentless. Though they haven't found what they're looking for, they have succeeded in disarming the palace police and have detained and interrogated eighteen staff members who, incredibly, do not reveal anything.

Hirohito is completely severed from the world. The Imperial Palace's great stone walls, a haven for so long, have now become a prison. For the first time in his entire life, there is no one to pamper him, pander to him, or protect him. Like the Japanese soldiers who died in island caves across the Pacific, Hirohito can only wait, unsure if he will live to see the morning.

At 3:00 A.M., forces loyal to the emperor storm the palace. Hatanaka and his allies flee into the night, having never found Hirohito or the recordings. Within hours they will take their own lives rather than face the consequences of their actions.

At 7:21 A.M., less than fifteen minutes after Harry Truman has received the message of Japanese surrender in Washington, D.C., the NHK broadcasts a special message: the emperor will speak directly to his people at noon.

CHAPTER 55

THE WHITE HOUSE WASHINGTON, D.C.

August 14, 1945 • 7:00 P.M.

THE OVAL OFFICE is thirty-six feet long and twenty-nine feet wide, and every square inch is taken up by a scrum of journalists, klieg lights, and newsreel cameras.

Wearing a navy blue double-breasted suit and blue shirt, the president stands at his desk to alert the world: "I have received this afternoon a message from the Japanese government," Truman begins, holding a copy of his speech in his right hand. "I deem this reply a full acceptance of the Potsdam Declaration which specifies the unconditional surrender of Japan."

Outside the White House, almost half a million Americans begin a massive street party in Washington. "This capital city . . .

Crowds that have gathered outside the White House react to the news of the Japanese surrender.
[Harry S. Truman Library]

relaxed its worn nerves and celebrated the winning of the war with a screaming, drinking, paper-tearing, free-kissing demonstration which combined all the features of New Year's and Mardi Gras," *Yank* magazine will report.

Truman himself, accompanied by his wife, Bess, steps onto the White House lawn. "We want Truman," the crowds lining the black wrought-iron fence chant. "We want Truman."

The president responds by holding up the two-fingered V-for-Victory sign.

At long last, World War II is over.

President Harry S. Truman announces to reporters that Japan has surrendered. First lady Bess Truman is seated on the couch, second from left.
[Harry S. Truman Library]

CHAPTER 56

TOKYO, JAPAN

August 15, 1945 • Noon

IN JAPAN, A TIME of national mourning has begun. At noon, as Washington celebrates, Emperor Hirohito's radio address is broadcast to cities, hamlets, and villages throughout the country. Japanese soldiers abroad also hear the message via shortwave radio. The people have never before heard the emperor's voice, so they react with a mixture of curiosity and shock. They are confused because the poor recording quality and the emperor's use of an archaic form of Japanese make him hard to understand. But eventually the message becomes clear.

"To our good and loyal subjects," the emperor starts in his high-pitched voice. "After pondering deeply the general trends of the world and the actual conditions obtaining in our empire today, we

Japanese POWs on Guam react to Emperor Hirohito's announcement of Japan's unconditional surrender, August 15, 1945. [National Archives]

have decided to effect a settlement of the present situation by resorting to an extraordinary measure. . . .

"The war has lasted for nearly four years. Despite the best that has been done by everyone—the gallant fighting of our military and naval forces, the diligence and assiduity of our servants of the State, and the devoted service of our one hundred million people—the war situation has developed not necessarily to Japan's advantage, while the general trends of the world have all turned against her interest."

Hirohito does not use the word "surrender." He merely states that he had resolved to "pave the way for a grand peace for all the generations to come by enduring the [unavoidable] and suffering what is unsufferable." To many, that is actually an enormous relief; their fathers, husbands, and sons might finally return home from the fighting. But other Japanese citizens are shamed and angry. Hirohito ends this address the Japanese never thought they would hear:

"Unite your total strength to be devoted to the construction for the future. Cultivate the ways of rectitude, nobility of spirit, and work with resolution so that you may enhance the innate glory of the Imperial State and keep pace with the progress of the world."

• • •

Across Japan, the truth sinks in: defeat. Many of the emperor's subjects are so stunned at the sound of Hirohito's voice admitting surrender that they collapse to the ground in shock. Several hundred military men kill themselves rather than accept Hirohito's capitulation. A group of army and navy officers opt to make their suicides public, kneeling on the gravel in front of the Imperial Palace before placing pistols to their heads.

In some cases, the Japanese response takes the form of rage, as more than a dozen captured American fliers are taken from their POW cells on the island of Kyushu and executed with swords. It is due to war crimes like these that almost as soon as Hirohito's speech is concluded, military bureaucrats across Japan begin burning files and documents that could be used against them by American investigators.

And so it is that Japan, the once-mighty occupying power, will itself now be occupied. Not even the god-man Hirohito can prevent that. Will the Americans seek vengeance? Will the conquerors destroy the Japanese way of life?

No one is sure, nor does anyone know how the Japanese will respond to their subjugation.

What is apparent is that a new emperor will soon arrive.

All hail General Douglas MacArthur.

CHAPTER 57

TOKYO BAY, JAPAN

August 29, 1945

PRESIDENT TRUMAN HAS DECIDED that the formal Japanese surrender will take place not on land but at sea. The Japanese leadership will sign the articles of surrender in Tokyo Bay, aboard the battleship USS *Missouri*. Dignitaries from all around the world will crowd the decks, MacArthur prominently among them.

Now, in a massive show of force, almost three hundred battleships, destroyers, cruisers, light aircraft carriers, frigates, sloops, submarines, tenders, hospital ships, and minesweepers wait their turn to sail through the minefields guarding the entrance to Tokyo Bay. In addition to the American fleet, there are ships from the navies of Britain, Australia, and New Zealand. If the people of

The USS Missouri *in 1945.* [Mary Evans Picture Library]

Japan have any doubt that they are defeated, they need only stand on the shore and stare out to sea.

Among the many vessels, the most powerful is Admiral William Halsey's flagship, the USS *Missouri*. Each of her sixteen-inch guns is sixty-seven feet in length, capable of launching a 2,700-pound armor-piercing shell twenty-three miles in less than fifty seconds. In addition, the Mighty Mo has twenty five-inch guns with an accurate range of ten miles. She is a monster of a ship, almost as long as a football field, with a crew of two thousand and a top speed of thirty-three knots. The *Missouri*'s big guns have fired on Iwo Jima, Okinawa, the Philippines, and Japan itself. Six months ago, the ship endured a direct hit by kamikaze attack. She absorbed the blow without loss of life.

There are also symbolic factors that add to the *Missouri*'s stature: The slate-gray vessel is named for the home state of President Harry Truman. His daughter, Margaret, actually shattered the champagne bottle across her bow when she was nearly twenty and he was still a senator, officially launching the *Missouri* from Brooklyn's naval shipyard in January 1944. An American flag that once flew over the United States Capitol in Washington is securely stored on board, waiting to be hoisted this coming Sunday. In addition, a second set of colors will be presented on board the *Missouri*: the thirty-one-star American flag belonging to Commodore Matthew Perry, whose historic 1853 voyage to Japan opened Japanese ports to American trade.

The *Missouri* is also the last battleship that the United States of America will ever build.

Early on the morning of August 29, 1945, a Japanese harbor pilot boards the *Missouri* to help Halsey's crew navigate the minefields and channels of Tokyo Bay. The pilot helps Quartermaster Third Class Ed Kalanta steer the 44,560-ton *Missouri* from the conning tower on the main bridge. It was Kalanta who drove the *Missouri* through the Panama Canal a year ago, sliding her into the narrow locks with just a foot to spare on either side. Now, Admiral Halsey is one floor below the main bridge as the nineteen-year-old Kalanta and his Japanese adviser masterfully guide her into Tokyo Bay, en route to her appointment with destiny.

● ● ●

The *Missouri* drops anchor at midmorning. Rehearsals soon begin for the surrender ceremony, as the ship's crew struggles to find space to fit the two hundred members of the press and dozens of dignitaries from around the world. History will take place on Sunday morning at 9:00 A.M. sharp.

Throughout the days of rehearsals, the *Missouri*'s mighty guns remain trained on Tokyo.

The war may be over, but the danger is not past.

CHAPTER 58

USS *MISSOURI* TOKYO BAY, JAPAN

September 2, 1945

ENERAL DOUGLAS MACARTHUR steps past Admiral Halsey and takes his place at the microphone shortly after 9:00 A.M. on Sunday, September 2. He is dressed in a crisp khaki uniform, as are the other American admirals and generals. The eleven-member Japanese contingent is wearing military dress and even formal top hats and tails, but it is MacArthur's rationale that "we fought them in our khaki uniforms, and we'll accept their surrender in our khaki uniforms."

The two thousand members of the USS *Missouri*'s crew, however, are all in their dress whites. They literally hang off gun turrets and other parts of the ship to witness this moment of history. The

deck is packed with media, dignitaries, and weapons of war. The sky is gray on this storm-tossed morning, and the mood somber.

"We are gathered here, representatives of the major warring powers, to conclude a solemn agreement whereby peace may be restored," MacArthur announces over the loudspeaker. "The issues, involving divergent ideals and ideologies, have been determined on the battlefields of the world, and hence are not for our discussion or debate."

The morning begins with the playing of "The Star-Spangled Banner." The thirty-one-star Commodore Perry flag from 1853 hangs in a frame affixed to the ship's superstructure, too fragile to snap smartly in the wind. The same cannot be said, however, for the Capitol flag, which was run up the flagpole this morning. The Japanese contingent looks morose and seems to want to conclude the ceremony as quickly as possible. The generals among them have already suffered the disgrace of surrendering their swords, and the diplomats had the Japanese flag removed from their official cars just this morning.

"As Supreme Commander for the Allied Powers, I announce it my firm purpose, in the tradition of the countries I represent, to proceed in the discharge of my responsibilities with justice and tolerance, while taking all necessary dispositions to ensure that the terms of surrender are fully, promptly, and faithfully complied with."

MacArthur clutches a sheaf of notes. He stands tall before the table on which the surrender will be signed.

Sailors hang off the turrets to watch the surrender ceremony on the USS Missouri.
[Mary Evans Picture Library]

Foreign Minister Mamoru Shigemitsu and General Yoshijiro Umezu lead the Japanese delegation that will sign the surrender agreement on board the USS Missouri *in Tokyo Bay.* [Harry S. Truman Library]

"I now invite the representatives of the emperor of Japan and the Japanese government and the Japanese Imperial General Headquarters to sign the instrument of surrender at the places indicated."

Japanese Foreign Minister Mamoru Shigemitsu signs the surrender agreement.
General MacArthur stands at the microphone. [National Archives]

A coffee-stained, dark green cloth covers a folding table brought up this morning from the ship's galley when it became clear that the ceremonial mahogany table donated by the British for the surrender ceremony would be too small. Two copies of the surrender agreement lie on the table, leather-bound for the Americans and canvas-covered for the Japanese. The surrender documents are printed on rare parchment found in a Manila basement.

The vanquished sign first, followed by the victors. Clicking camera shutters are the only sound as the crew and press eagerly capture the moment. The ceremony lasts twenty-three minutes and is broadcast around the world.

General Douglas MacArthur takes his seat at the table in a simple wooden chair and patiently begins using a series of different fountain pens to affix his name twice. He hands one pen to Lieutenant General John "Skinny" Wainwright, his dear friend who spent the war in a Japanese POW camp after being captured during the fall of the Philippines. The sight of the skeletal Wainwright evokes the beatings, torture, and starvation to which he was subjected for three years as a prisoner of war.

Another ceremonial pen is handed to Lieutenant General Arthur Percival, a British commander who also endured the horrors of a Japanese POW camp after the fall of Singapore. Like Wainwright, Percival was moved several times by the Japanese to prevent him from falling into Allied hands. By war's end, Percival and Wainwright were held at the same prison in Hsian, Manchuria. MacArthur has specifically asked these two bone-thin,

General Douglas MacArthur signs the Japanese surrender agreement. Lieutenant General Jonathan Wainwright and Lieutenant General A. E. Percival, both former POWs, stand behind him. [National Archives]

malnourished survivors to stand immediately behind the surrender table, visible at all times to the Japanese party.

The ceremony concluded, MacArthur rises to his feet, stands ramrod straight, and announces to all in attendance that "these proceedings are closed."

As the Japanese are led back to the motor launch that will carry them to land, a formation of American aircraft flies overhead. Looking up, the vanquished receive a dramatic message: the Americans are now your masters.

U.S. Army and Navy planes fly in formation over the USS Missouri *at the conclusion of the Japanese surrender ceremony.* [Harry S. Truman Library]

AMERICAN EMBASSY TOKYO, JAPAN

September 27, 1945 • 10:00 A.M.

A NERVOUS AND PREOCCUPIED Emperor Hirohito steps out of his maroon 1930 Rolls-Royce at the entrance of the American embassy in Tokyo. The emperor's war is not over. Hirohito is depressed, and his hands tremble. He suffers from severe jaundice, which has deepened the sallow pallor of his skin. Last night he lay awake worrying that he will have to stand in a prisoner's dock, listening to an American prosecutor listing his many war crimes.

Taking a deep breath, Hirohito momentarily calms his fears. Perhaps he won't hang, after all. His only hope is a direct appeal to General Douglas MacArthur, which is why the emperor has traveled to the American embassy this morning. Courage is everything right now, even if it is false.

The emperor could have saved himself days of worry by greeting MacArthur a week ago. Hirohito's Imperial Palace is just across a moat from MacArthur's brand-new office headquarters in Tokyo's Dai-Ichi Seimei Building. When MacArthur moved in, he gave the Dai-Ichi Life Insurance Company three days to vacate the imposing structure, then chose for himself a simple sixth-floor office that actually looks down onto the Imperial Palace.

But while Hirohito can see MacArthur's office just by looking out the window, and MacArthur can just as easily see him, the emperor has waited for MacArthur to make the first move. But the general is cunning. Paying a call upon the emperor would have been seen as subservient. Better to have it the other way around.

MacArthur has designated that the meeting should take place at the American embassy, allowing the people of Tokyo plenty of opportunity to see the emperor's unmistakable car making the shameful drive to MacArthur's residence. The emperor's journey from the Sakurada-mon Gate of the Imperial Palace south through the decimated streets of Tokyo has taken less than ten minutes. His imperial sedan has been followed by three black Mercedes loaded with members of the royal court, but the emperor pays little attention to them now.

Clad in a black waistcoat, top hat, and polished dress shoes, Hirohito steps through the American embassy's front door. He is unused to commoners touching his personal possessions, and immediately recoils as two army officers salute him and then step forward to take his hat.

"You are very, very welcome, sir!" says a grinning MacArthur, striding into the room to break the ice. He wears his usual khaki uniform rather than formal wear and has not even affixed his combat ribbons to the simple pressed shirt. The general thrusts out his hand to greet the emperor, but Hirohito bows low at the same time, leaving MacArthur's open hand hovering awkwardly above the emperor's head. Hirohito continues to bow, finally extending his hand upward to clasp MacArthur's.

After a moment's hesitation, MacArthur invites Hirohito and his interpreter into a private room. The two men speak for forty minutes. The emperor apologizes for the war—an admission MacArthur actually downplays during their conversation.

This is the first of eleven meetings that will take place between MacArthur and Hirohito over the next several years, but it is the most important. For in this simple midmorning conversation, MacArthur makes it clear that he sees the emperor as vital to forging an alliance that will successfully rebuild Japan. Even though the emperor's admission of culpability makes him a war criminal, MacArthur will do everything in his considerable power to make sure Hirohito never sees the inside of a jail cell—or feels the coarse braid of a hangman's noose around his throat.

At the meeting's end, MacArthur's personal photographer is shown into the room. It was Captain Gaetano Faillace who snapped the iconic image of the general wading ashore in the Philippines six months ago, and now he snaps another photo for the ages. Faillace actually takes three pictures of MacArthur and Hirohito standing side by side in front of a desk. In the first two, MacArthur's eyes are closed and Hirohito appears to be yawning. But the third image, the one that will forever remind the Japanese people that their emperor no longer rules Japan, is the keeper.

The six-foot MacArthur towers over Hirohito, looking dominant and unimpressed by the small man to his left. The emperor stands at stiff attention; MacArthur looks casual, hands on his hips and elbows sticking out from his sides.

Just to make sure the message is received loud and clear, MacArthur orders that the photo be released to the newspapers so that all of Japan can see the towering American who now rules their nation.

Predictably, the people of Japan are horrified.

Three months later, on January 1, 1946, at MacArthur's urging, Emperor Hirohito denies his divine status, admitting to the people of Japan that he is not a god.

Thus, the divine nature of the Japanese ruler is revealed as a fraud—but that admission comes far too late for the millions of dead scattered across Asia.

General Douglas MacArthur, commander of the American occupation of Japan, meets with Emperor Hirohito at the U.S. embassy in Tokyo, September 1945. [Harry S. Truman Library]

AFTERWORD

THE OCCUPATION OF JAPAN:
TURNING AN ENEMY INTO AN ALLY

I N THE MONTHS FOLLOWING the Japanese surrender, American soldiers and sailors poured into Japan by the thousands, disarming the Japanese military, disabling naval guns, and removing the propellers from airplanes. The long, slow process of healing the great divide between America and Japan began. In China, forty thousand U.S. Marines served garrison duty and accepted the surrender of Japanese units that had not yet fallen to the Soviets. Many Japanese forces in China had never before suffered defeat in battle; the act of laying down their arms and ceremonially burning their regimental flags was bitter and humiliating.

Between 1945 and 1952, enormous changes took place in Japan. Emperor Hirohito was allowed to remain the symbolic figure representing Japanese unity and culture, but a legislature was set up with elected representatives to make all decisions in the country; women were given the right to vote; and the Japanese military was dismantled. The country was forbidden to form a military or ever go to war again.

On April 28, 1952, the American occupation of Japan was ended through a treaty signed in San Francisco in 1951, and peace was formally declared between Japan and forty-eight nations that signed the treaty.

The U.S. Pacific Fleet in Tokyo Bay after the surrender of Japan. Mount Fuji, an active volcano and the highest mountain in Japan, appears in the background. [Harry S. Truman Library]

THE DECISION TO DEVELOP AND USE THE BOMB
LETTER FROM ALBERT EINSTEIN TO FDR

IN 1933 AFTER THE NAZIS came to power in Germany, Albert Einstein immigrated to the United States. The German physicist, whose famous equation opened the door to nuclear fission, understood that as a Jew he would be persecuted in his homeland. In 1939, his fame well established, Einstein succeeded in getting his thoughts about a bomb, and Germany's experiments to build one, into the hands of President Franklin Roosevelt.

Old Grove Rd.
Nassau Point
Peconic, Long Island

August 2nd, 1939

F.D. Roosevelt,
President of the United States,
White House
Washington, D.C.

Sir:

Some recent work by E. Fermi and L. Szilard, which has been communicated to me in manuscript, leads me to expect that the element uranium may be turned into a new and important source of energy in the immediate future. Certain aspects of the situation which has arisen seem to call for watchfulness and, if necessary, quick action on the part of the Administration. I believe therefore that it is my duty to bring to your attention the following facts and recommendations:

In the course of the last four months it has been made probable—through the work of Joliot in France as well as Fermi and Szilard in America—that it may become possible to set up a nuclear chain reaction in a large mass of uranium, by which vast amounts of power and large quantities of new radium-like elements would be generated. Now it appears almost certain that this could be achieved in the immediate future.

This new phenomenon would also lead to the construction of

bombs, and it is conceivable—though much less certain—that extremely powerful bombs of a new type may thus be constructed. A single bomb of this type, carried by boat and exploded in a port, might very well destroy the whole port together with some of the surrounding territory. However, such bombs might very well prove to be too heavy for transportation by air.

The United States has only very poor ores of uranium in moderate quantities. There is some good ore in Canada and the former Czechoslovakia, while the most important source of Uranium is Belgian Congo.

In view of this situation you may think it desirable to have some permanent contact maintained between the Administration and the group of physicists working on chain reactions in America. One possible way of achieving this might be for you to entrust with this task a person who has your confidence and who could perhaps serve in an inofficial capacity. His task might comprise the following:

a) to approach Government Departments, keep them informed of the further development, and put forward recommendations for Government action, giving particular attention to the problem of securing a supply of uranium ore for the United States;

b) to speed up the experimental work, which is at present being carried on within the limits of the budgets of University laboratories, by providing funds, if such funds be required, through his contacts with private persons who are willing to make a contribution for this cause, and perhaps also by obtaining the co-operation of industrial laboratories which have the necessary equipment.

I understand that Germany has actually stopped the sale of uranium from the Czechoslovakian mines which she has taken over. That she should have taken such early action might perhaps be understood on the ground that the son of the German Under-Secretary of State, von Weizsäcker, is attached to the Kaiser-Wilhelm-Institut in Berlin where some of the American work on uranium is now being repeated.

Yours very truly,
(Albert Einstein)

[Source: FDR Presidential Library]

GENERAL EISENHOWER'S THOUGHTS

THE LIST OF MILITARY leaders who opposed the use of the atomic bomb is long. Most felt that Japan was near surrender. General Dwight Eisenhower reflected the feelings of many. In his book *Mandate for Change*, he recalls the feeling when Secretary of War Henry Stimson informed him that the bomb was about to be used:

In 1945 . . . Secretary of War Stimson, visiting my head-quarters in Germany, informed me that our government was preparing to drop an atomic bomb on Japan. I was one of those who felt that there were a number of cogent reasons to question the wisdom of such an act. . . . The Secretary, upon giving me the news of the successful bomb test in New Mexico, and of the plan for using it, asked for my reaction, apparently expecting a vigorous assent.

During his recitation of the relevant facts, I had been conscious of a feeling of depression and so I voiced to him my grave misgivings, first on the basis of my belief that Japan was already defeated and that dropping the bomb was completely unnecessary, and secondly because I thought that our country should avoid shocking world opinion by the use of a weapon whose employment was, I thought, no longer mandatory as a measure to save American lives. It was my belief that Japan was, at that very moment, seeking some way to surrender with a minimum loss of "face." The Secretary was deeply perturbed by my attitude.

PRESIDENT TRUMAN'S REFLECTIONS

THE DECISION TO USE the bomb was the president's alone. Harry Truman wrote at length about the decision in his memoirs. In this letter written around the eighteenth anniversary of the attack on Hiroshima and Nagasaki, he sums up his thoughts. He is writing to a journalist at the *Chicago Sun-Times* who had written a favorable article about Truman's decision.

[Source: Harry S. Truman Library/NARA]

HARRY S. TRUMAN
INDEPENDENCE, MISSOURI
August 5, 1963

Dear Kup:

I appreciated most highly your column of July 30th, a copy of which you sent me.

I have been rather careful not to comment on the articles that have been written on the dropping of the bomb for the simple reason that the dropping of the bomb was completely and thoroughly explained in my Memoirs, and it was done to save 125,000 youngsters on the American side and 125,000 on the Japanese side from getting killed and that is what it did. It probably also saved a half million youngsters on both sides from being maimed for life.

You must always remember that people forget, as you said in your column, that the bombing of Pearl Harbor was done while we were at peace with Japan and trying our best to negotiate a treaty with them.

All you have to do is to go out and stand on the keel of the Battleship in Pearl Harbor with the 3,000 youngsters underneath it who had no chance whatever of saving their lives. That is true of two or three other battleships that were sunk in Pearl Harbor. Altogether, there were between 3,000 and 6,000 youngsters killed at that time without any declaration of war. It was plain murder.

I knew what I was doing when I stopped the war that would have killed a half million youngsters on both sides if those bombs had not been dropped. I have no regrets and, under the same circumstances, I would do it again - and this letter is not confidential.

Sincerely yours,

Harry Truman

Mr. Irv Kupcinet
Chicago Sun-Times
Chicago, Illinois

LETTERS AND OPINIONS FROM SUBSEQUENT PRESIDENTS

ALL LIVING FORMER PRESIDENTS were asked by Bill O'Reilly to give their opinions about President Truman's decision to drop the A-bomb. Presidents George H. W. Bush and Jimmy Carter, former navy men, share their thoughts below, along with President George W. Bush. Each agrees with Truman's decision. (Presidents Bill Clinton and Barack Obama declined to give their opinions of Truman's actions.)

James Earl Carter, a midshipman at the U.S. Naval Academy, was considered to be an active-duty serviceman during the war. He entered Annapolis in 1943 and graduated with the class of 1946. If the war had not ended, Carter would most certainly have been sent to the Pacific with his classmates as part of the invasion that would have been launched against Japan. Carter later served on the USS *Mississippi*, a battleship that had seen extensive service in the Pacific theater. In 1948, he transitioned to submarines, where he trained to be the engineering officer on one of the first nuclear submarines. Jimmy Carter resigned from the navy in 1953 after his father died.

JIMMY CARTER

    This is an excerpt from "A Full Life." I haven't changed my mind.

"We… were again at sea about a year later, when we sat on deck and listened to President Truman's nasal voice announce over the loudspeaker that a formidable weapon had been dropped on Hiroshima and that he hoped this would convince the Japanese to surrender. All of us agreed with his decision, because it was generally believed that 500,000 Americans would have been lost in combat and many more Japanese killed if we had invaded the Japanese homeland and it was defended with suicidal commitment by Japanese troops on the ground. We were disappointed when we didn't return to port in time to join in the celebration when Japan surrendered just a few days later."

        Sincerely,

        Jimmy Carter

George H. W. Bush joined the navy in 1942 on his eighteenth birthday, earning his wings as a naval aviator before he turned nineteen. He was assigned to the Pacific on the aircraft carrier USS *San Jacinto*, where he flew fifty-eight combat missions during the war. On September 2, 1944, exactly one year before the Japanese surrender, he was forced to bail out when his Avenger torpedo bomber was hit by enemy flak. Bush parachuted to safety, spending four hours afloat on a life raft before being rescued by an American submarine. In December 1944, after fifteen months of combat duty, he was reassigned to the naval training station in Norfolk, Virginia, where he served as a flight instructor until his release from the navy upon the Japanese surrender in September 1945.

President George W. Bush offered his opinion on President Truman's decision.

GEORGE BUSH

January 5, 2016

Dear Bill,

In response to your question, I think Harry Truman did the right thing. Thousands of Americans would have died invading Japan. Maybe even me. My squadron was training for the invasion and close to shipping out again when Harry dropped the bomb. So would I have done the same thing? I think so. At that time, it was the right decision. Tough but right.

I hope this helps. Happy New Year.

Sincerely,

G Bush

Mr. Bill O'Reilly
Anchor
Fox News Channel
1211 Avenue of the Americas
17th Floor
New York, NY 10036-8795

GEORGE W. BUSH

February 9, 2016

Mr. Bill O'Reilly
New York, New York

Dear Bill:

Thank you for writing about this consequential time in our
Nation's history, and thanks for asking my opinion.

When Harry Truman took office suddenly in the final months of
World War II, he said, "I felt like the moon, the stars, and the all
the planets had fallen on me." Yet the man from Missouri knew
how to make a hard decision and stick by it.

In the presidency, there are no do-overs. You have to do what
you believe is right and accept the consequences. Harry Truman
did just that. I admire his toughness, principle, and strategic
vision. He led with our country's best interests at heart, and he
didn't care much what the critics said.

As an American and the son of a World War II veteran, I
support his decision and am grateful.

Sincerely,

George W. Bush

LITTLE BOY AND FAT MAN

LITTLE BOY

Fuel: Uranium

Weight: 9,700 lb. or 4.85 tons

Length: 120 inches

Diameter: 28 inches

Explosive force: 16,000 tons TNT equivalent

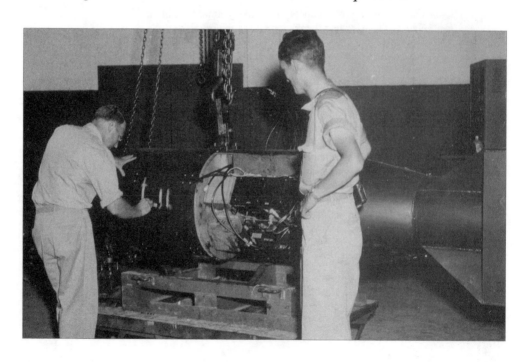

LITTLE BOY AND FAT Man were different kinds of bombs. A gun-like part fired into Little Boy's uranium to start the nuclear reaction. In Fat Man, the plutonium was surrounded by tons of explosives. Fat Man was the second plutonium bomb ever detonated. The first was the bomb used in the Trinity test in New Mexico on July 16, 1945.

FAT MAN

Fuel: Plutonium

Weight: 10,300 lb. or 5.15 tons

Length: 128 inches

Diameter: 60 inches

Explosive force: 21,000 tons TNT equivalent

HIROSHIMA AND NAGASAKI: IMMEDIATE AND LASTING EFFECTS

THE DETAILS OF THE DEATHS and injuries inflicted by Little Boy and Fat Man are horrific. In both cases, 90 percent of the people within sixteen hundred feet of the strikes died instantly. Of those within one mile from the strikes, more than two-thirds were injured and at least one-third of those eventually died of their injuries.

We will never know how many people in both cities were instantly evaporated.

The bombs exploded and sent fire and heat waves in all directions. Many victims had excruciating flash burns over their faces and hands and other skin exposed when their clothing burned away. Thousands of others were crushed in the buildings they were in, or fatally cut by glass projectiles as they tried to escape. Radiation released by the bombs penetrated deep into human tissue and injured cells. It was often hard to know if one had radiation sickness until hair began to fall out or skin became discolored. Many who lived would discover they had cancer as many as thirty years after the bombings.

The total deaths from the bombings of Hiroshima and Nagasaki will never be known. It was impossible to keep records in the chaos. Although possibly conservative, these numbers are generally agreed upon.

Hiroshima: 90,000–130,000 dead by December 1945
Nagasaki: 60,000–80,000 dead by December 1945

The effects of the atomic bombs on Hiroshima and Nagasaki were felt for decades. Both cities have been rebuilt in remarkable fashion, with almost all buildings possessing the same concrete-and-steel construction as the structures that survived the initial blasts. In Hiroshima, the Genbaku Dome was the only building

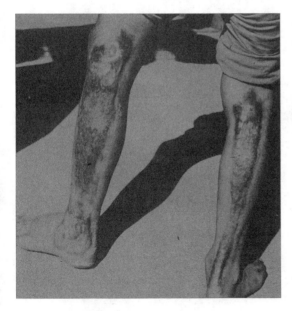

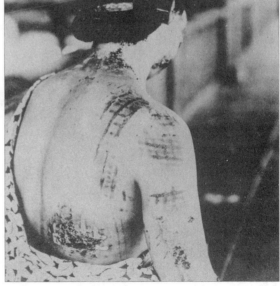

People were terribly burned from the atomic heat and radiation unleashed by the bombs in Japan.
[National Archives]

This photograph shows burns in the pattern of the kimono the woman was wearing at the time of the explosion. [National Archives]

left standing beneath the center of the blast. Preserved today as part of the Hiroshima Peace Memorial, it has become the most enduring symbol of the first atomic bomb. The T-shaped Aioi Bridge, which served as *Enola Gay*'s aiming point, survived the bombing and remained in place for several years afterward. However, structural damage caused by the A-bomb eventually took its toll, and the bridge was rebuilt.

Nagasaki is less than four hours by bullet train to the southwest of Hiroshima. The rugged nature of the countryside is a subtle reminder that the Operation Olympic invasion would have required overcoming very formidable terrain. Nagasaki's bustling port and dockland are a popular port of call for cruise lines, cargo ships, and Japanese naval vessels. A large monument of polished stone two miles by streetcar from downtown Nagasaki marks the A-bomb's hypocenter, the ground directly beneath the bomb's explosion. (It's a stark contrast to the Hiroshima hypocenter, a small plaque located in an alley, with the words "Enola Gay" misspelled as "Enora Gay.")

Like Hiroshima, Nagasaki does not define itself by the atomic bomb. But both cities are tourist sites because of the explosions and have museums detailing the bombs' damage.

The Genbaku Dome in Hiroshima was the only large structure remaining after the atomic bomb was dropped. Today it is part of the Hiroshima Peace Memorial, a UNESCO world heritage site. [Mary Evans Picture Library]

PEARL HARBOR

OR YEARS, THE JAPANESE military had known its primary adversary might eventually be the United States. Knowing a long war would be disastrous for Japan, the commander in chief of Japan's Combined Fleet, Admiral Isoroku Yamamoto, with the support of Prime Minister Tojo, favored a surprise preemptive attack that would destroy the U.S. Pacific Fleet, the "dagger being pointed at our throats," and force the Americans into an agreement that would allow Japan free rein in East Asia.

He devised an audacious attack plan. It would happen on a Sunday morning, a time when most sailors would be sleeping in after a night on the town. Waves of carrier-launched Japanese planes would drop from the skies, unloading torpedoes and bombs that would sink destroyers and demolish airplanes, forever ending America's naval presence in the Pacific.

Yamamoto knew just where to find these ships. They were anchored bow to stern and side by side at a balmy tropical U.S. naval base near Honolulu, Hawaii—a place known as Pearl Harbor.

On November 8, 1941, Prime Minister Tojo presented Emperor Hirohito with specific details about the surprise attack. After very little deliberation, he approved the plan.

An aerial view of Pearl Harbor in October 1941. [National Archives]

On December 7, 1941, at 7:55 A.M. Hawaii time, hundreds of Japanese planes appeared in the skies. In less than ninety minutes, they destroyed or damaged 328 airplanes and nineteen naval vessels, including eight enormous battleships. More than twenty-four hundred Americans lost their lives. The attack was a complete surprise. The eight battleships were the *Nevada, Arizona, West Virginia, Oklahoma, Pennsylvania, Tennessee, Maryland,* and *California.* Five were sunk in the attack, along with the target ship *Utah.* The *Nevada, West Virginia,* and *California* were later refloated and returned to service; the *Oklahoma* was raised but was damaged beyond repair and scrapped. The wreckage of the USS *Arizona* and USS *Utah* can still be seen today on the floor of Pearl Harbor, memorials to the men who died. The bodies of the sailors within have never been removed.

The day after the attack, President Roosevelt asked Congress to declare war on Japan.

President Roosevelt signs the declaration of war against Japan, December 8, 1941. [National Archives]

SHAME ON AMERICAN SOIL: RELOCATION CENTERS

AS THE SHOCK OF PEARL HARBOR settled across America, citizens became suspicious of anything associated with Japan. On February 19, 1942, President Roosevelt, citing wartime necessity, signed Executive Order 9066. The order authorized the removal of Japanese Americans from the West Coast, which had

Children of Japanese ancestry play baseball at the Santa Anita Assembly Center, an internment camp in Arcadia, California, April 6, 1942. [National Archives]

been declared a military zone. Having committed no crime other than having ancestors from Japan, more than 120,000 people were taken to relocation centers and kept against their will. At least seventy thousand of them were U.S. citizens.

Entire families were rounded up and sent to live for the duration of the war in ten camps in isolated areas of Arizona, Arkansas, California, Colorado, Idaho, Utah, and Wyoming. Most people were kept for two to three years, sleeping side by side in barracks surrounded by barbed-wire fences. Armed guards looked down from high sentry towers, scrutinizing their every movement.

FDR'S "DAY OF INFAMY" SPEECH
DECEMBER 8, 1941

YESTERDAY, DECEMBER 7, 1941—*a date which will live in infamy—the United States of America was suddenly and deliberately attacked by naval and air forces of the Empire of Japan.*

The United States was at peace with that nation and, at the solicitation of Japan, was still in conversation with its Government and its Emperor looking toward the maintenance of peace in the Pacific. Indeed, one hour after Japanese air squadrons had commenced bombing in Oahu, the Japanese Ambassador to the United States and his colleague delivered to the Secretary of State a formal reply to a recent American message. While this reply stated that it seemed useless to continue the existing diplomatic negotiations, it contained no threat or hint of war or armed attack.

It will be recorded that the distance of Hawaii from Japan makes it obvious that the attack was deliberately planned many days or even weeks ago. During the intervening time the Japanese

Government has deliberately sought to deceive the United States by false statements and expressions of hope for continued peace.

The attack yesterday on the Hawaiian Islands has caused severe damage to American naval and military forces. Very many American lives have been lost. In addition American ships have been reported torpedoed on the high seas between San Francisco and Honolulu.

Yesterday the Japanese Government also launched an attack against Malaya. Last night Japanese forces attacked Hong Kong. Last night Japanese forces attacked Guam. Last night Japanese forces attacked the Philippine Islands. Last night the Japanese attacked Wake Island. This morning the Japanese attacked Midway Island.

Japan has, therefore, undertaken a surprise offensive extending throughout the Pacific area. The facts of yesterday speak for themselves. The people of the United States have already formed their opinions and well understand the implications to the very life and safety of our nation.

As Commander-in-Chief of the Army and Navy, I have directed that all measures be taken for our defense.

Always will we remember the character of the onslaught against us. No matter how long it may take us to overcome this premeditated invasion, the American people in their righteous might will win through to absolute victory.

I believe I interpret the will of the Congress and of the people when I assert that we will not only defend ourselves to the uttermost but will make very certain that this form of treachery shall never endanger us again.

Hostilities exist. There is no blinking at the fact that our people, our territory and our interests are in grave danger.

With confidence in our armed forces—with the unbounded determination of our people—we will gain the inevitable triumph—so help us God.

I ask that the Congress declare that since the unprovoked and dastardly attack by Japan on Sunday, December seventh, 1941, a state of war has existed between the United States and the Japanese Empire.

[Source: The National D-Day Museum]

EMPEROR HIROHITO'S
SURRENDER SPEECH
THE "JEWEL VOICE" BROADCAST
AUGUST 15, 1945

To OUR GOOD and loyal subjects: After pondering deeply the general trends of the world and the actual conditions obtaining in our empire today, we have decided to effect a settlement of the present situation by resorting to an extraordinary measure.

We have ordered our Government to communicate to the Governments of the United States, Great Britain, China and the Soviet Union that our empire accepts the provisions of their joint declaration.

To strive for the common prosperity and happiness of all nations as well as the security and well-being of our subjects is the solemn obligation which has been handed down by our imperial ancestors and which we lay close to the heart.

Indeed, we declared war on America and Britain out of our sincere desire to insure Japan's self-preservation and the stabilization of East Asia, it being far from our thought either to infringe upon the sovereignty of other nations or to embark upon territorial aggrandizement.

But now the war has lasted for nearly four years. Despite the best that has been done by everyone—the gallant fighting of our military and naval forces, the diligence and assiduity of our servants of the State, and the devoted service of our one hundred million people—the war situation has developed not necessarily to Japan's advantage, while the general trends of the world have all turned against her interest.

Moreover, the enemy has begun to employ a new and most cruel bomb, the power of which to do damage is, indeed, incalculable, taking the toll of many innocent lives. Should we continue to fight, it would not only result in an ultimate collapse and obliteration of the Japanese nation, but also it would lead to the total extinction of human civilization.

Such being the case, how are we to save the millions of our subjects, or to atone ourselves before the hallowed spirits of our imperial ancestors? This is the reason why we have ordered the acceptance of the provisions of the joint declaration of the powers.

We cannot but express the deepest sense of regret to our allied nations of East Asia, who have consistently cooperated with the Empire toward the emancipation of East Asia.

The thought of those officers and men as well as others who have fallen in the fields of battle, those who died at their posts of duty, or those who met death [otherwise] and all their bereaved families, pains our heart night and day.

The welfare of the wounded and the war sufferers and of those who lost their homes and livelihood is the object of our profound solicitude. The hardships and sufferings to which our nation is to be subjected hereafter will be certainly great.

We are keenly aware of the inmost feelings of all of you, our subjects. However, it is according to the dictates of time and fate that we have resolved to pave the way for a grand peace for all the generations to come by enduring the [unavoidable] and suffering what is unsufferable. Having been able to safeguard and maintain the structure of the Imperial State, we are always with you, our good and loyal subjects, relying upon your sincerity and integrity.

Beware most strictly of any outbursts of emotion that may engender needless complications, of any fraternal contention and strife that may create confusion, lead you astray and cause you to lose the confidence of the world.

Let the entire nation continue as one family from generation to generation, ever firm in its faith of the imperishableness of its divine land, and mindful of its heavy burden of responsibilities, and the long road before it. Unite your total strength to be devoted to the construction for the future. Cultivate the ways of rectitude, nobility of spirit, and work with resolution so that you may enhance the innate glory of the Imperial State and keep pace with the progress of the world.

[Source: Federal Communications Commission]

JAPANESE WAR CRIMES TRIALS

BOTH JAPANESE AND AMERICAN forces committed horrendous acts in the name of winning the war. General Curtis LeMay believed that if America had lost, his decision to firebomb Tokyo would most certainly have seen him indicted for war crimes. But it is the victor who metes out final punishment. Just as the Nazi leadership went on trial in Nuremberg, so too were Japan's generals held accountable for their acts of terror.

Twenty-eight of the country's top military and political leaders were charged with Class A crimes against peace, in other words, waging an aggressive war. Twenty-five were convicted; seven were sentenced to death. In addition, Allied prosecutors held tribunals against thousands of Japanese generals, government officials, soldiers, and camp guards throughout Asia and the Pacific. Forty-three hundred were found guilty of rape, abuse of POWs, and murder. About a thousand of those men were sentenced to death, and hundreds were given life imprisonment.

On May 3, 1946, the world began to hear the list of atrocities committed by Prime Minister Hideki Tojo and the troops under his control, beginning with the cold-blooded murders of millions of Chinese civilians and surrendered soldiers and thousands of

Allied prisoners of war. In one incident during the Second Sino-Japanese War, after the Japanese army conquered the town of Nanking in China and the Chinese troops fled, Tojo's men remained and killed three hundred thousand civilians in a six-week bloodbath. The International Military Tribunal for the Far East decreed that he should be hanged by the neck until dead. On December 22, 1948, that sentence was carried out.

International judges at the war crimes trials in Tokyo, May 12, 1946.
[Harry S. Truman Library]

THE NUCLEAR WORLD

TODAY, NINE NATIONS have nuclear weapons: the United States, Russia, the United Kingdom, France, China, India, Israel, Pakistan, and North Korea. In all, it is estimated there are 15,350 nuclear weapons in existence. The weapons are developed and stored largely as deterrents to warfare. None have been used in any war since World War II. The United States and Russia cooperate to reduce and limit each country's supply, as agreed upon in New START, the New Strategic Arms Reduction Treaty. Many experts feel that nuclear weapons are not useful in the kinds of political struggles that exist in the twenty-first century, ones that take place in extreme terrains and busy cities, against small groups of enemy.

AFTER THE WAR

EMPEROR **HIROHITO** WAS STRIPPED of all power by General Douglas MacArthur. However, the general felt that Hirohito was symbolically vital to healing the nation's postwar wounds. Therefore, MacArthur quietly decreed that Hirohito be absolved of all responsibility for war crimes. To maintain the ruse that the emperor was not directly involved in the war effort and its many atrocities, MacArthur and Hirohito collaborated to slant testimony of the war crimes defendants away from the emperor.

In recent decades, revisionist historians in Japan have repudiated the notion that the emperor is not divine, suggesting that the wording of Hirohito's pronouncement was a vague gesture to placate the American occupiers. "The occupation forces tried to sever the bond between the emperor and the Japanese people," reads a museum display at Tokyo's controversial Yasukuni Shrine. "They widely advertised the new year statement as the 'emperor's declaration of humanity,' but in actuality the emperor had done no more than to announce a return to the principles stated in Emperor Meiji's [1868] charter oath."

Hirohito made a point of boycotting the Yasukuni Shrine, in the heart of Tokyo, when he learned in 1978 that fourteen Japanese war criminals had secretly been added to the list of souls honored there. In the four decades between the war's end and his death, Hirohito appeared regularly in public, greeting foreign heads of state during their visits to Tokyo and traveling abroad to meet with both Queen Elizabeth of the United Kingdom and U.S. President Gerald Ford. Emperor Hirohito died on January 7, 1989, at the age of eighty-seven, after reigning for sixty-two years.

Joseph Stalin established communist governments in Eastern Europe and maintain control by imprisoning dissenters. The Soviet Union developed an atomic bomb and exploded it in a test August 29, 1949, becoming the second nuclear nation in the world. Stalin died on March 5, 1953, and his body was on view in a mausoleum in Red Square for eight years before it was buried.

Robert Oppenheimer became world famous once the atomic bombs were dropped and details of the Manhattan Project were released to the public. He appeared on the cover of both *Time* and *Life* magazines as the intellectual face of the dawning nuclear age. Oppenheimer tried to return to the academic world, but realized that his passion for teaching had waned. He accepted a position as director of a think tank known as the Institute for Advanced Study.

He became an advocate for nuclear arms control and opposed the development of the hydrogen bomb, which was successfully tested in 1952. These new thermonuclear weapons explode with a force exponentially greater than the Hiroshima and Nagasaki blasts. They actually require an atomic reaction to trigger the greater thermonuclear detonation, leading to the saying, "All nuclear weapons are atomic, but not all atomic weapons are nuclear."

During the anticommunist era of the 1950s, Robert Oppenheimer was accused of being an agent for the Soviet Union, and his security clearance was suspended. After a hearing in 1954, the Atomic Energy Commission found no evidence of treason, but called him a security risk nonetheless and stripped him of his clearance altogether. A later examination of declassified files would show that Oppenheimer never betrayed the United States and had resisted several attempts by the Soviet KGB to recruit him as a spy. However, this revelation came long after Oppenheimer's death from throat cancer on February 18, 1967, at the age of sixty-two.

Albert Einstein was granted U.S. citizenship in 1940. Although his letter to FDR led to the formation of the Manhattan Project, he was not allowed to be involved. The FBI thought that Einstein's status as an avowed pacifist with liberal sympathies made him too great a security risk. FBI director J. Edgar Hoover maintained a secret file on Einstein but was never able to prove that the physicist had communist ties. Many of Einstein's friends took part in the project, and they made him well aware of its ongoing progress.

In 1947, Einstein was working with the Emergency Committee of Atomic Scientists, based in Princeton, New Jersey. As part of that group, he penned a letter that reads in part:

"We scientists believe upon ample evidence that the time of decision is upon us—that what we do or fail to do within the next few years will determine the fate of our civilization. . . .

"In the shadow of the atomic bomb, it has become apparent that all men are brothers. If we recognize this as truth and act upon this recognition, mankind may go forward to a higher plane of human development. If the angry passions of a nationalistic world engulf us further, we are doomed."

Albert Einstein died in 1955 from an aortic aneurysm at the age of seventy-six. His body was cremated, but only after his brain had been removed without permission by a Princeton Hospital pathologist so that it might be studied for science.

Colonel Paul Tibbets was dogged by controversy about the Hiroshima bombing for the rest of his life. However, he never backed down from his belief that he had done the right thing. The *Enola Gay* itself became an unlikely lightning rod for controversy when the Smithsonian's National Air and Space Museum in Washington, D.C., refurbished it after many years of neglect and planned to display it for the fiftieth anniversary of the war's end. Workers spent two decades and more than three hundred thousand man-hours restoring the plane to its original condition. The exhibit would have questioned the decision to use the bombs. Under pressure from veterans' groups, the exhibit was altered to allow visitors to come up with their own interpretation of the ethics of dropping the bomb. The *Enola Gay* is now displayed at the National Air and Space Museum's Steven F. Udvar-Hazy Center in Chantilly, Virginia.

Bockscar, which dropped the atomic bomb on Nagasaki, has also been lavishly restored. It is currently on display at the National Museum of the U.S. Air Force at Wright-Patterson Air Force Base near Dayton, Ohio.

Both Colonel Tibbets of *Enola Gay* and **Major Charles**

Sweeney of *Bockscar* were promoted to general during their long military careers. Tibbets stayed in the air force and proved instrumental in pioneering the transition to jet-powered bomber flight. Sweeney left active duty after the Second World War but continued to fly in the Massachusetts Air National Guard. Sweeney died in Boston in 2004, at the age of eighty-four. Tibbets lived to be ninety-two years old and requested that he be cremated so that protesters might not make his grave site a rallying point for antinuclear demonstrations. His ashes were scattered over the English Channel, over which he had flown many times during World War II.

On June 25, 1950, communist North Korea invaded U.S.-backed South Korea. Soon after, **General Douglas MacArthur** was named commander of the United Nations forces there, charged with repelling the communist advance. The general successfully launched one of history's greatest amphibious invasions in September 1950, sending waves of troops ashore far behind enemy lines at Inchon and recapturing the South Korean capital of Seoul.

In response to this success, MacArthur was authorized to conduct limited operations in North Korea. A confident MacArthur, however, sent half his army north, expanding the conflict in an effort to reunify the Korean peninsula and eliminate the communists. China intervened, beating the American-led U.N. forces back south, but again MacArthur drove into North Korea. By spring of 1951, while President Truman was preparing to negotiate peace, MacArthur was campaigning to expand the war into China.

Truman decided MacArthur had to go. By this time,

MacArthur's immense popularity made the decision to fire him a political liability, but Truman was unfazed. Calling a meeting of his top advisers on April 6, he broached the topic of dismissing the vaunted general. At stake was the question of whether or not civilian authorities had a say in military policy. It was clear that MacArthur planned to fight the war in Korea and China on his terms, without heed to the authority of the president of the United States.

The Joint Chiefs of Staff soon weighed in, favoring the dismissal of MacArthur for insubordination. On April 7, Truman wrote in his journal of the Joint Chiefs that "it is the unanimous opinion of all that MacArthur be relieved. All four so advise."

On April 11, 1951, when Truman formally announced that he was relieving MacArthur of command, there was an enormous public outcry of support for the general. Truman's public opinion rating once again tanked. Nevertheless, at 8:00 P.M. Washington time on April 11, MacArthur was sacked. Truman had authorized his secretary of the army, Frank Pace Jr., to deliver the news, but Pace did not receive the order. Instead, MacArthur heard about his firing on the radio while eating lunch with his wife in Tokyo.

This marked the end of Douglas MacArthur's military career. He returned home a hero, feted by a ticker-tape parade in New York City viewed by seven million people. More than three thousand tons of paper were dropped from windows, balconies, and rooftops.

Douglas MacArthur lived out the rest of his life in luxury, with his wife and son in a penthouse atop the Waldorf Astoria Hotel in

New York City. In 1962, he gave his legendary "Duty, Honor, Country" speech at West Point, concluding with the words:

"The shadows are lengthening for me. The twilight is here. My days of old have vanished, tone and tint. They have gone glimmering through the dreams of things that were. Their memory is one of wondrous beauty, watered by tears, and coaxed and caressed by the smiles of yesterday. I listen vainly, but with thirsty ears, for the witching melody of faint bugles blowing reveille, of far drums beating the long roll. In my dreams I hear again the crash of guns, the rattle of musketry, the strange, mournful mutter of the battlefield. But in the evening of my memory, always I come back to West Point. Always there echoes and re-echoes: Duty, Honor, Country. Today marks my final roll call with you, but I want you to know that when I cross the river my last conscious thoughts will be of the Corps, and the Corps, and the Corps. I bid you farewell."

Douglas MacArthur died on April 5, 1964. He was eighty-four years old. Before burial, his body lay in state in the Capitol Rotunda in Washington, D.C., where an estimated 150,000 people waited in line to pay their respects.

Harry Truman did not run for a third term in office. He returned to his beloved Independence, Missouri, and became Mr. Citizen. He read, lectured, took long walks, and visited with guests and neighbors. Truman died on December 26, 1972, at the age of eighty-eight; his wife, Bess, died ten years later. Both are buried at his presidential library in Independence, Missouri.

TIME LINE

September 18, 1931: Japan invades Manchuria.

July 12, 1937: Conflict between China and Japan escalates into an undeclared war.

September 1, 1939: Germany invades Poland, beginning World War II.

October 11, 1939: President Roosevelt receives Albert Einstein's letter about the bomb.

October 18, 1941: Hideki Tojo becomes Japanese prime minister after Fumimaro Konoe resigns.

December 7, 1941: Japan bombs Pearl Harbor in Hawaii and attacks the Philippines, Wake Island, Guam, Malaya, Thailand, Shanghai, and Midway.

December 8, 1941: The United States and England declare war on Japan. Japan invades the Philippines.

December 9, 1941: China declares war on Japan.

December 23, 1941: General Douglas MacArthur initiates a withdrawal from Manila to Bataan.

December 27, 1941: Japan bombs Manila.

February 19, 1942: FDR signs Executive Order 9066 allowing the roundup and incarceration of Japanese American citizens.

February 22, 1942: General MacArthur is ordered to evacuate to Australia.

March 18, 1942: FDR appoints General MacArthur Allied commander of the Southwest Pacific Area.

April 9, 1942: The remaining U.S. and Filipino troops in the Philippines surrender and are forcibly marched sixty-five miles to a prison camp. The march becomes known as the Bataan Death March.

June 4–7, 1942: The United States defeats Japan at the Battle of Midway.

August 7, 1942: U.S. troops begin their assault at Guadalcanal.

December 1, 1942: U.S. government acquires the Los Alamos Ranch School in New Mexico.

December 31, 1942: Emperor Hirohito gives permission for his troops to evacuate Guadalcanal.

Oct. 5–6, 1943: The United States bombs Japanese positions on Wake Island.

October 7, 1943: The Japanese execute ninety-eight American civilian contractors on Wake Island.

July 24, 1944: U.S. Marines invade Tinian Island.

September 15–November 27, 1944: U.S. Marines suffer sixty-five hundred casualties in capturing Peleliu.

October 20, 1944: General MacArthur wades ashore on Leyte Island, leading the U.S. Sixth Army invasion to recapture the Philippines.

October 23–26, 1944: The U.S. Navy scores a decisive victory in the Leyte Gulf.

October 25, 1944: First Japanese kamikaze attack.

February 3, 1945: Allied troops begin the fight for Manila.

February 4–11, 1945: Franklin Roosevelt, Winston Churchill, and Joseph Stalin meet at Yalta to discuss postwar Europe and the Soviet Union's entry into war in the Pacific.

February 19–March 26, 1945: U.S. Marines capture Iowa Jima; nearly seven thousand Americans are killed in the battle.

March 3, 1945: U.S. and Filipino troops take Manila.

March 10, 1945: Two hundred seventy-nine U.S. B-29s drop 1,665 tons of napalm bombs on Tokyo.

April 1–June 23, 1945: More than twelve thousand Americans are killed and fifty thousand are wounded in the Battle of Okinawa; an estimated 150,000 Japanese die, including civilians.

April 12, 1945: President Franklin Roosevelt dies. Harry Truman becomes president.

May 7, 1945: Germany surrenders, ending the war in Europe.

May 8, 1945: Victory in Europe Day.

July 5, 1945: General MacArthur declares the Philippines liberated.

July 16, 1945: Trinity test is successful in New Mexico.

July 17, 1945: Truman, Churchill, and Stalin meet in Potsdam, Germany, to continue Yalta discussions on reconstruction of Europe and the further prosecution of war against Japan.

July 26, 1945: The Potsdam Declaration defining the terms of Japanese surrender is issued. Parts for the bomb Little Boy are unloaded on Tinian Island.

July 25, 1945: General Dwight Eisenhower is informed of the Trinity test.

August 1, 1945: General MacArthur is briefed about the planned bombings.

August 6, 1945: The first atomic bomb is dropped on Hiroshima.

August 9, 1945: The second atomic bomb is dropped on Nagasaki.

August 14, 1945: Japan accepts unconditional surrender.

September 2, 1945: Formal surrender ceremony on the USS *Missouri* in Tokyo Bay.

THE AUTHOR RECOMMENDS

Recommended Reading

Ambrose, Stephen E. *The Good Fight: How World War II Was Won.* New York: Atheneum Books for Young Readers, 2001.

Black, Wallace. *Island Hopping in the Pacific.* New York: Crestwood House, 1992.

Houston, Jeanne Wakatsuki, and James D. Houston. *Farewell to Manzanar: A True Story of Japanese American Experience During and After the World War II Internment.* Boston, MA: Houghton Mifflin, 1973.

Marrin, Albert. *The Airman's War: World War II in the Sky.* New York: Atheneum, 1982.

Perl, Lila. *Behind Barbed Wire.* New York: Benchmark Books, 2003.

Sandler, Martin. *Why Did the Whole World Go to War? And Other Questions About World War II.* New York: Sterling Children's Books, 2013.

Sheinkin, Steve. *Bomb: The Race to Build—and Steal—the World's Most Dangerous Weapon.* New York: Roaring Brook Press, 2012.

Stanley, Jerry. *I Am an American: A True Story of Japanese Internment.* New York: Crown Publishers, 1994.

Stein, R. Conrad. *World War II in the Pacific.* Berkeley Heights, NJ: Enslow, 2002.

World Book. *World War II in the Pacific.* Chicago: World Book, 2011.

Recommended Viewing

PLEASE NOTE: Watching the events that took place at the end of World War II in the Pacific may be much harder than reading about them. Sensitive viewers should watch with an adult or ask an adult to preview the news clips.

Most of the strategic events of May through September 1945 were recorded live. A YouTube search for these key terms will lead you to the film clips. As always, watch the clips that are presented by trustworthy institutions such as the U.S. War Department, PBS, the BBC, and the Naval History and Heritage Command (navy.mil).

- Enola Gay
- Hiroshima
- "Remembering the Tragic Aftermath of the Hiroshima Bomb"
- "President Truman announces the bombing of Hiroshima 1945"
- Robert Oppenheimer
- Douglas MacArthur

AUTHOR'S SOURCE NOTES

A GREAT DEAL OF THE joy in writing a work of history comes from the detective investigation required to flesh out an episode or a subject and make it rise up off the page. Travel, archival searches, governmental databases, websites, and the works of other authors are just a few of the resources that we rely upon. The author wishes to thank James Zobel at the MacArthur Memorial Foundation in Norfolk, Virginia, for his tireless help in tracking down obscure documents pertaining to the general and his life. Visitors to Norfolk are encouraged to pay this underappreciated museum a visit, for it offers an abundance of information about MacArthur's life as well as a vast number of his personal effects.

Head Archivist Dara Baker at the Naval War College was most helpful in tracking down the movements of Admiral Nimitz through the document known as the Nimitz Graybook. David Clark at the Harry S. Truman Library & Museum in Independence, Missouri, was also very helpful in finding some of the more obscure details of the late president's life. As with all presidential libraries, the Truman Library's website offers exhaustive detail about his presidency and lifelong habit of letter writing. The papers of a great number of lesser Truman administration officials can also be found there. Visit www.trumanlibrary.org to have a look.

The U.S. Naval Academy Museum in Annapolis, Maryland, should be a required stop for anyone with even a passing interest in history, showcasing the United States Navy—and so much more. The exhibits visitors can view include the spur belonging to John Wilkes Booth that caught on patriotic bunting as he leaped from the presidential box after shooting President Abraham Lincoln, and the tomb of the legendary John Paul Jones. For this book, we were interested in the displays detailing the navy's impact on the Pacific war as well as a large number of artifacts, including the pen Admiral Chester Nimitz used to sign the Japanese surrender documents and a sword surrendered by the Japanese delegation to the Allies on the morning of September 2, 1945. Also on display at the Naval Academy Museum are a number of flags that have played prominent roles in American naval history, including the Stars and Stripes flown by Commodore Matthew Perry when he sailed into Tokyo Bay in 1853 and later displayed on board the USS *Missouri* on the morning of the Japanese surrender. The USNA Museum is also in possession of the other American flag that flew aboard the *Missouri*, but it is not currently on display. Thank you to archivist Jim Cheevers for his assistance.

There is a fine Pearl Harbor display and film at the USNA Museum, but for the greatest effect, readers are encouraged to visit the USS Arizona Memorial in Honolulu, Hawaii. In addition to looking around a detailed museum and watching a vivid film detailing the attack and its aftereffects, visitors can travel by boat to the spot in the harbor where the *Arizona* still rests. Many of the men who died when she exploded and sank that Sunday morning are still entombed inside the ship. Many of those who survived the attack have requested that upon their deaths, their ashes be placed within the *Arizona* so that they might be laid to rest with their former shipmates.

On display nearby, positioned so that its guns symbolically protect the memorial and the men of the *Arizona*, is the USS *Missouri*. The Mighty Mo is a museum ship now, and visitors can come aboard to see the precise spot on which the Japanese surrender documents were signed.

The author would also like to thank the Smithsonian's National Air and Space Museum in Washington, D.C., and distinguished World War II writer and researcher Brian Sobel.

● ● ●

What follows are other resources utilized in this writing. This list is by no means exhaustive but will provide the readers with a road map to use in their own historical investigations.

Websites, Newspapers, and Archives: General Background Information

News Sources: *New York Times, Life* magazine, *Los Angeles Times,* the *Guardian, Washington Post, Spokane Daily Chronicle, Australian, Wall Street Journal, Times of India,* Associated Press, *U.S. News &*

World Report, *New Yorker*, *Japan Times*, *New York Post*, *Chicago Tribune*, *Marine Corps Chevron*, Fox News, PBS, BBC.

Websites: Architect of the Capitol (www.aoc.gov); Office of the Clerk, U.S. House of Representatives (www.clerk.house.gov); National Archives (www.archives.gov), especially dated February 26, 1945, entitled "Captured Japanese Instructions Regarding the Killing of POW"; Battle of Manila Online (www.battleofmanila .org); Congressional Medal of Honor Society (www.cmohs.org); Supreme Court of the United States (www.supremecourt.gov); FBI Records—The Vault (https://vault.fbi.gov); U.S. Department of State—Office of the Historian (history.state.gov); Central Intelligence Agency (www.cia.gov); USS *Indianapolis* (www.ussindiana polis.org); Bulletin of the Atomic Scientists (www.thebulletin.org), especially Ellen Bradbury and Sandra Blakeslee, "The Harrowing Story of the Nagasaki Bombing Mission."

Archives: Franklin D. Roosevelt Presidential Library and Museum; United States National Archives; Princeton University Library, The Manhattan Project—U.S. Department of Energy; The George C. Marshall Foundation; U.S. Department of State— Office of the Historian; Library of Congress—Carl Spaatz Papers; Congressional Record, V. 145, Pt. 8, May 24, 1999, to June 8, 1999; Congressional Record, V. 146, Pt. 15, October 6, 2000, to October 12, 2000; National Library of Australia—Trove (archives of the *Argus*); U.S. Naval War College (especially the Nimitz Graybook); Harry S. Truman Library & Museum; Records of the United States Marine Corps; U.S. Naval Institute *Naval History* Archive;

U.S. Army Center of Military History: Combat Chronicles of U.S. Army Divisions in World War II.

Peleliu

Adam Makos with Marcus Brotherton, *Voices of the Pacific*; E. B. Sledge, *With the Old Breed*; John C. McManus, *Grunts*; John Toland, *The Rising Sun: The Decline and Fall of the Japanese Empire, 1936–1945*; Major Frank O. Hough, USMC, *The Assault on Peleliu*.

MacArthur

Douglas MacArthur, *Reminiscences*; Samuel Eliot Morison, *History of United States Naval Operations in World War II*, vol. 13: *The Liberation of the Philippines—Luzon, Mindanao, the Visayas, 1944–1945*; Robert Ross Smith, *Triumph in the Philippines (United States Army in World War II: The War in the Pacific)*; Gavin Long, *MacArthur*.

Truman

Jon Taylor, *Harry Truman's Independence: The Center of the World*; Sean J. Savage, *Truman and the Democratic Party*; David M. Jordan, *FDR, Dewey, and the Election of 1944*; Jules Witcover, *No Way to Pick a President*; Margaret Truman, *Harry S. Truman*; Steven Lomazow and Eric Fettman, *FDR's Deadly Secret*; Leslie R. Groves, *Now It Can Be Told: The Story of the Manhattan Project*; Thomas Fleming, *Truman*; David McCullough, *Truman*; Margaret Truman, *Bess W. Truman*; Steve Neal, ed., *Eleanor and Harry: The Correspondence of Eleanor Roosevelt and Harry S. Truman*;

J. Samuel Walker, *Prompt and Utter Destruction: Truman and the Use of Atomic Bombs Against Japan*.

Hirohito and Japan
Arne Markland, *Black Ships to Mushroom Clouds: A Story of Japan's Stormy Century 1853–1945*; Francis Pike, *Hirohito's War: The Pacific War, 1941–1945*; Herbert P. Bix, *Hirohito and the Making of Modern Japan*; Michael Kort, *The Columbia Guide to Hiroshima and the Bomb*; D. M. Giangreco, *Hell to Pay: Operation Downfall and the Invasion of Japan, 1945–1947*; Douglas J. MacEachin, *The Final Months of the War with Japan*; Tsuyoshi Hasegawa, ed., *The End of the Pacific War: Reappraisals*; Hutton Webster, *Rest Days: The Christian Sunday, the Jewish Sabbath, and Their Historical and Anthropological Prototypes*; Edward J. Drea, *In the Service of the Emperor: Essays on the Imperial Japanese Army*; Noriko Kawamura, *Emperor Hirohito and the Pacific War*; Gavan Daws, *Prisoners of the Japanese: POWs of World War II in the Pacific*; E. Bartlett Kerr, *Surrender and Survival: The Experience of American POWs in the Pacific, 1941–1945*; David M. Glantz, *Soviet Operational and Tactical Combat in Manchuria, 1945: "August Storm"*; Stephen Harding, *Last to Die: A Defeated Empire, a Forgotten Mission, and the Last American Killed in World War II*.

Air Corps
Robert Frank Futrell, *Ideas, Concepts, Doctrine: Basic Thinking in the United States Air Force, 1907–1960*; Samuel Russ Harris Jr., *B-29s Over Japan, 1944–1945: A Group Commander's Diary*; James G.

Blight and Janet M. Lang, *The Fog of War: Lessons from the Life of Robert S. McNamara*; Edwin P. Hoyt, *Inferno: The Fire Bombing of Japan, March 9–August 15, 1945*; Graham M. Simons, *B-29: Superfortress: Giant Bomber of World War 2 and Korea*; Robert O. Harder, *The Three Musketeers of the Army Air Forces: From Hitler's Fortress Europa to Hiroshima and Nagasaki*; Eric Larrabee, *Commander in Chief: Franklin Delano Roosevelt, His Lieutenants and Their War*.

Trinity and Atomic Bombs

Everett M. Rogers and Nancy R. Bartlit, *Silent Voices of World War II*; Robert James Maddox, ed., *Hiroshima in History: The Myths of Revisionism*; Gar Alperovitz et al., *The Decision to Use the Atomic Bomb*; Robert Cowley, ed., *The Cold War: A Military History*; Richard Rhodes, *The Making of the Atomic Bomb*; Michael D. Gordin, *Five Days in August: How World War II Became a Nuclear War*; Robert Jay Lifton, *Death in Life: Survivors of Hiroshima*; John Hersey, *Hiroshima*; Paul Ham, *Hiroshima Nagasaki: The Real Story of the Atomic Bombings and Their Aftermath*; Al Christman, *Target Hiroshima: Deak Parsons and the Creation of the Atomic Bomb*; Charles Pellegrino, *To Hell and Back: The Last Train from Hiroshima*; Gerard DeGroot, *The Bomb: A Life*; Tsuyoshi Hasegawa, ed., *The End of the Pacific War: Reappraisals*; Dennis D. Wainstock, *The Decision to Drop the Atomic Bomb: Hiroshima and Nagasaki: August 1945*; Ray Monk, *Robert Oppenheimer: A Life Inside the Center*; Samuel Glasstone, ed., *The Effects of Nuclear Weapons*.

USS Indianapolis and U.S. Navy

Richard F. Newcomb, *Abandon Ship!: The Saga of the U.S.S.* Indianapolis, *the Navy's Greatest Sea Disaster*; Doug Stanton, *In Harm's Way: The Sinking of the U.S.S.* Indianapolis *and the Extraordinary Story of Its Survivors*; Edwyn Gray, *Captains of War: They Fought Beneath the Sea*; Christopher Chant, *The Encyclopedia of Code Names of World War II*; Raymond B. Lech, *The Tragic Fate of the U.S.S.* Indianapolis: *The U.S. Navy's Worst Disaster at Sea*; Walter R. Borneman, *The Admirals: Nimitz, Halsey, Leahy, and King— the Five-Star Admirals Who Won the War at Sea*; Kit Bonner and Carolyn Bonner, *USS* Missouri *at War*.

Additional Sources

Brown University. *Hiroshima: Ending the War Against Japan: Science, Morality, and the Atomic Bomb.* 5th ed. July 2007. The Choices Program. www.choices.edu

Chaliand, Gérard. *The Art of War in World History.* Berkeley, CA: University of California Press, 1994.

Eggenberger, David. *An Encyclopedia of Battles.* New York: Dover, 1985.

Hersey, John. "Hiroshima." *The New Yorker*, August 31, 1946.

Kelly, Cynthia C. *The Manhattan Project: The Birth of the Atomic Bomb in the Words of Its Creators, Eyewitnesses, and Historians.* New York: Black Dog & Leventhal, 2009.

O'Reilly, Bill, and Martin Dugard. *Killing the Rising Sun: How America Vanquished World War II Japan.* New York: Henry Holt, 2016.

Sheinkin, Steve. *Bomb: The Race to Build—and Steal—the World's Most Dangerous Weapon.* New York: Roaring Brook, 2012.

Truman, Harry S. *Memoirs: 1945 Year of Decisions.* Vol. 1. Reprint, New York: William S. Konecky, 1999.

INDEX

Alamogordo Army Air Field, 78
Allied forces, in Europe, xiv, 94
Allied forces, in Pacific, xii, xiv, 7
Allison, Sam, 68
Alvarez, Luis, 170
American Embassy, Tokyo, Japan, 237–40
Americans
  on atomic bomb, 169–71
  Japanese, 263–64
Anami, Korechika, 206
antipersonnel bombs, 14
Arnold, Hap, 51, 105
Ashworth, Frederick, 189, 194–95
atomic bombs
  Americans on, 169–71
  B-29 bombers and, 42–43
  building of, 6, 41–42
  Eisenhower on, 94, 96, 105, 246–47
  Fat Man bomb, 123, 186–200, 255, *255*
  Groves and, xii, *xiii*, 4–5, 61–62, 67, *70*
  Handy and, 103
  Little Boy bomb, 71–73, *72*, 76, 113–15, *122*, 128–33, 136–47, 254, *254*
  MacArthur and, 103–6, 168
  Manhattan Project and, xii, 2–6, *3*, 41–43, 58–69, *70*, 88
  opposition to, 94, 96, 103–5, 168
  order to drop, 103–6
  Parsons, W., on, 124
  radiation from, 77, 201
  Roosevelt, F., on, 88
  Spaatz and, 102–3
  Stimson on, 105
  targets of, 42–43, 91, 104, 120
  testing of, 39, 42, 58–69, *59*, *60*, *70*, 76–78
  Trinity, 58–69, *70*, 76–78, 126–27
  Truman, H., on, 39–40, 81, 88, 91, 247–48
  U.S. presidents on, 249–53
Augusta, USS, 157–61

B-29 bombers
  atomic bombs and, 42–43
  Big Stink, 191–92
  Bockscar, 186–99, *187*, 277–78
  crewmen on, 118–23
  Enola Gay, 115, *129*, 129–33, 277–78
  The Great Artiste, 190–92, 195, 198
  in Hiroshima, 107–12
  in Kure bombings, 82, *84*, 84–85
  in Tokyo bombings, 24, 26–31, *27*
Baldwin, Hanson, 170
balloon bombs, 14
Bard, Ralph A., 105
Battle of the Bulge, 16
Beahan, Kermit, 193–95, 197
Berlin, Germany, 79–91, *89*
Big Stink, 191–92
Birch, A. F., *72*
Bockscar, *187*, 277–78
  crewmen on, *193*, 193–99
  Fat Man bomb and, 186–99
  Sweeney and, 188–99
  Tibbets and, 190, 191

Buckley, Edward K., 194
Bunker Hill, USS, *52*
Bush, George H. W., 251, 252
Bush, George W., 251, 253
Byrnes, James, 211

Carter, James Earl, 249–50
Cavert, Samuel McCrea, 204
China. *See* Manchuria conflict
Churchill, Winston, xiv, *xv*
  in Potsdam summit, 61, *80*, 87–93, *90*
  in Yalta conference, 15–19, *16*, *17*
Clinton, Bill, 249

"Day of Infamy Speech," 265–67
D-Day invasion, 7
DeBernardi, Louie, 71
Dehart, Albert, 194–95
Doolittle, Jimmy, 199
Doolittle raid, 199

Early, Steve, 35–36
Eatherly, Claude, 120
Einstein, Albert, xiv, *xv*
  Roosevelt, F., and, xvi–xvii, 243–46
  after World War II, 276–77
Eisenhower, Dwight D., xiv, *xiv*, 106,
    165–66
  on atomic bombs, 94, 96, 105, 246–47
  D-Day invasion and, 7
Enola Gay
  dropping of Little Boy by, 136–42
  Hiroshima and, *115*, *129*, 129–33,
    136–42, 277–78

Faillace, Gaetano, 11, 239–40
Farrell, Thomas F., 68
Fat Man bomb, 123, *189*
  Bockscar and, 186–99
  diagram of, *188*
  dropping of, 186–200
  overview of, 255, *255*

Ferebee, Thomas, 138–40
Ford, Gerald, 275
Forrestal, James, 211, 212
France, 7
fukkaku strategy, 99

Genbaku Dome, 257–59, *258*
Geneva Conventions, 172–73
Germany. *See also* Potsdam summit
  atomic bomb attempts of, 6
  Berlin, 79–91, *89*
  Hitler and, 44
  invasion of, 16
  surrender of, 44, 210
Graham, Frank H., 158–59
The Great Artiste, 190–92, 195, 198
Groves, Leslie
  in Los Alamos, 2
  Manhattan Project and, xii, *xiii*, 4–5,
    61–62, 67, *70*
Guadalcanal, 44, 46

Hague Conventions, 172–73
Halsey, William, 227–28
Handy, Thomas, 102–3
Hanford Engineer Works, 78
Hatanaka, Kenji, 216–17
Hensel, H. Struve, 96
Hirohito, xii, *xiii*, *33*, *54–55*, 116–17, 120,
    207
  Hiroshima and, 162–64
  on Japanese military defense, 53, 56
  during Japanese surrender, 205–17, 221,
    223, 237–40, *240*, 268–70
  on Leyte, Visayan Islands, 13–14
  MacArthur and, 237–40, *240*, 274
  after Manchuria invasion, 178–80
  Nagasaki and, 205–8
  surrender speech by, 221, 223,
    268–70
  during Tokyo bombings, 31, 32
  after World War II, 241–42, 274–75

Hiroshima
  B-29 bombers in, 107–12
  bombing of, 91, 107–15, 128–47, *148–53*
  description of, 112
  destruction of, after bombing, 141–47,
    145–46, 148–53
  Enola Gay and, *115, 129,* 129–33,
    136–42, 277–78
  Genbaku Dome in, 257–59, *258*
  Hirohito and, 162–64
  immediate and lasting effects of, 181,
    184–85, 256–59
  Imperial Palace after bombing of, 162–64
  Lewis and, 133, 140
  Little Boy bomb and, 71–73, *72,* 76,
    113–15, *122,* 128–33, 136–47, 254, *254*
  MacArthur and, 165–68
  map of destruction in, *146*
  news on, 156, 170, 172–73
  post-attack mosaic of, *182–83*
  pre-attack mosaic view of, *108–9*
  Sweeney in, 190–91
  as target, 91, 112
  Truman, H., after, 157–61
  warnings to, 110–12, *111*
Hitler, Adolf, 44
Hopkins, James I., 192
Hunter's Point, San Francisco, California,
  71–73

Imperial Guard, 216–17
Imperial Japanese Army, 216
Imperial Japanese Navy, 53, 98
Imperial Palace, 13–14, 31, 53, *54–55,* 56,
  116–17
  after Hiroshima bombing, 162–64
  during Japanese surrender, 216–17
  after Manchuria invasion, 178–80
Indianapolis, USS, 71–73, 76
internment camps. *See* relocation centers
Iwo Jima, Japan, 14, *22,* 46, 99, 120, 124,
  186, 227

Japan, xii, xvii. *See also* Hiroshima; Nagasaki
  American Embassy, Tokyo, Japan, 237–40
  atomic bomb attempts of, 6
  Geneva Conventions and, 172–73
  Hague Conventions and, 172–73
  Imperial Japanese Army, 216
  Imperial Japanese Navy, 53, 98
  Imperial Palace in, 13–14, 31, 53, *54–55,*
    56, 116–17
  Iwo Jima, 14, *22,* 46, 99, 120, 124, 186,
    227
  kamikaze pilots from, 12, 48, 52, *98, 99*
  Kokura, 120, 191–95
  Kure bombings, 82–86, *84*
  Kyushu, 56, 96–97, 99–101
  Leyte, Visayan Islands and, 8–9, 13–14
  MacArthur, on invading, 51–52, 99–100
  major bombings in, *25*
  in Manchuria conflict, 18–19, 49, 116,
    174–78
  Manila, Philippines, and, 22–23, 51–52
  national morale in, 83–86
  occupation of, 241–42
  Okinawa Island, 14, 44–49, *45–47,* 57, *83,*
    99, 195, 198–99, 227
  Operation Olympic in, *95,* 96–97,
    99–101, 105–6
  Pearl Harbor and, xvii, 73, 204, 260–62
  Potsdam summit and, 61, *80,* 87–93, *90,*
    111–12, 210–12, 218
  Sasebo Naval Station in, 99
  Soviet Union and, 18–19
  Supreme Council for Direction of War in,
    117, 206–8
  Tokyo Bay, 225–36, *242*
  Tokyo bombings, March 10, 1945, 24–31
  Tokyo bombings, March 18, 1945, 32–34
  Toyama, 110
  war crimes by, 172–73, 224, 271–73, *274*
  Yasukuni Shrine in, 274–75
Japanese Americans, 263–64
Japanese messages and codes, *97,* 97–98

Japanese military defense
fukkaku strategy, 99
Hirohito on, 53, 56
Imperial Japanese Navy and, 53, 98
Ketsu-Go strategy, 85
military training and, 14
preparing for invasion, 98–99
Japanese prisoners of war, 85–86, *86, 222*
Japanese surrender, 205–8, 241–42
conditions of, 209–17
Hirohito during, 205–17, 221, 223,
237–40, *240,* 268–70
Imperial Palace during, 216–17
letter of, 209–12
news of, 216, 218–24, *219*
Potsdam summit and, 210–12, 218
refusal to surrender, 162–64, 168, 172,
178–80
revolts relating to, 216–17
surrender ceremony, on *Missouri,* 228–35
surrender speech, 221, 223, 268–70
in Tokyo Bay, 225–36, *242*
Truman, H., and, 209–14, 218–20, *220,*
225
Jeppson, Morris, 136–37
"Jewel Voice" broadcast, 268–70
Jornada del Muerto Desert, 42
atomic bomb testing in, 58–69, *59, 60, 70,*
76–78

kamikaze pilots, 12, 48, 52, *98, 99*
Ketsu-Go strategy, 85
King, Ernest, 51
Kistiakowsky, George, 69
Koiso, Kuniaki, xii, 13
Kokura, Japan, 120, 191–95
Kuharek, John D., 198
Kure bombings, 82–86, *84*
Kyushu, Japan, 56, 96–97, 99–101

Lawrence, David, 171
Leahy, William D., 105, 211

LeMay, Curtis, xiv, *xiv,* 26, 115, 190,
271
attacks by, 110–12
in Tokyo bombings, *30,* 31, 34
Lewis, Robert, 133, 140
Leyte, Visayan Islands
Hirohito on, 13–14
Japan and, 8–9, 13–14
MacArthur in, 7–12, *9*
Sutherland in, 10
Yamashita and, 13
Little Boy bomb
dropping of, 136–47
Hiroshima and, 71–73, *72,* 76, 113–15,
122, 128–33, 136–47, 254, *254*
mission for, 113–15
overview of, 254, *254*
preparation for dropping, 128–33
Tibbets and, 113–15, 118–25, *119,*
128–33, 136–42
Los Alamos, New Mexico. *See also*
Manhattan Project
Groves in, 2
Oppenheimer in, 2–6, 41–43
theater group in, 6

M-69 firebombs, 28–31, *29,* 34
MacArthur, Douglas, x, *xii, 167,* 210
in Allied Forces, xii, 7
atomic bombs and, 103–6
background on, 9
Hirohito and, 237–40, *240,* 274
Hiroshima and, 165–68
on invading Japan, 51–52, 99–100
Kyushu and, 56, 96–97, 99–101
in Leyte, Visayan Islands, 7–12, *9*
on Manchuria conflict, 176–77
in Manila, Philippines, 20–23, 51–52,
96–106, 165–68, 176–77
military strategy of, 99–100
on *Missouri,* 229–35, *235*
Nimitz and, 100

in Operation Olympic, *95*, 96–97,
  99–101, 105–6
Truman, H., and, 165–66
after World War II, 274, 278–80
Manchuria conflict, 18–19, 49
  invasion, by Soviet Union, 174–78
  MacArthur on, 176–77
  Stalin and, 116, 174
Manhattan Project
  atomic bomb testing by, 58–69
  Groves and, xii, *xiii*, 4–5, 61–62, 67, *70*
  location of, 2–6, *4, 5*
  Oppenheimer and, xii, 2–6, *3*, 41–43,
    58–69, *70*
  Roosevelt, F., on, 88
Manila, Philippines
  battle in, 21–23
  Japan and, 22–23, 51–52
  MacArthur in, 20–23, 51–52, 96–106,
    165–68, 176–77
  Spaatz in, 102–6
  Yamashita in, 22
Marquardt, George, 120
Marshall, George, 102, 105, 165–66
Matsushige, Yoshito, 144
McCloy, John J., 105
McIntire, Ross T., 96
McKnight, Charles, 120
McVay, Charles, III, xiv, *xv*, 73, 123
Mikami, Yosaku, 134–35
military strategy, 99–100. *See also*
    Japanese military defense
military training, 14
Missouri, USS
  description of, 227–28
  MacArthur on, 229–35, *235*
  surrender ceremony on, 228–35
  symbolic features of, 227
  in Tokyo Bay, 225–36, *226, 236*
Montgomery, Bernard, 16
Mori, Takeshi, 216
Moscow, Soviet Union, 49

Nagasaki
  Bockscar and, 186–99, *187*, 277–78
  bombing of, 91, 120, 186–202
  description of, 195, 197
  Hirohito and, 205–8
  immediate and lasting effects of bombing,
    200–202, 256–59
  Shinto shrine in, *202*
  Truman, H, after bombing of, 203–4
napalm, 28
Nashville, USS, 7, 10, 11
New Mexico. *See also* Manhattan Project
  Alamogordo Army Air Field in, 78
  Jornada del Muerto Desert in, 42, 58–69,
    59, 60, 70, 76–78
  Los Alamos, 2–6, 41–43
news and publicity, 10
  on Hiroshima, 156, 170, 172–73
  Japanese surrender, 216, 218–24, *219*
  after Trinity testing, 78
Nimitz, Chester, *xiii*, xiv, 104
  MacArthur and, 100
Nixon, Richard, 168
nuclear chain reactions, xvi–xvii, 137
nuclear weapons, 273. *See also* atomic bombs

Obama, Barack, 249
Okinawa Island
  battle in, 44–49, *45–47*, 57, 99
  casualties in, 46, 48
  description of, 46–48
  pictorial map of, *83*
  Stalin and, 49
  United States and, 14, 44–49, *45–47*, 57,
    83, 99, 198–99
Olivi, Fred, 198
Oneida, x
Operation Coronet, 100
Operation Magic, 98
Operation Meetinghouse, 28–31
Operation Olympic, *95*, 96–97, 99–101,
    105–6

Oppenheimer, Robert, *xiii*
  background on, 4–5
  in Los Alamos, 2–6, 41–43
  Manhattan Project and, xii, 2–6, *3*,
    41–43, 58–69, *70*
  Trinity atomic bomb testing and, 58–69,
    59, *70*
  after World War II, 275–76
O'Reilly, Angela, ix–x
O'Reilly, William James, Jr., ix–x, 249–53
O'Reilly, William James, Sr., ix–xi

Parsons, Bob, 124
Parsons, William "Deak," *119*, 123–24,
    128–29, 136–37
Patton, George S., xiv, *xv*, 16, 106
  on Soviet Union, 49
Pearl Harbor, xvii, 73, 204, 260–62
Peleliu, Philippines, 7, 8, 46–47, 99
Penney, William, 126
Percival, Arthur, 234–35, *235*
Perry, Matthew, 227
Philippines. *See* Leyte, Visayan Islands;
    Manila, Philippines; Peleliu,
    Philippines
plutonium, 76, 78, 190. *See also* Fat Man
    bomb
Potsdam summit
  Churchill in, 61, *80*, 87–93, *90*
  Japanese surrender and, 210–12, 218
  Stalin in, 61, *80*, *90*, 91–93
  Truman, H., in, 61, *80*, 87–93, *90*, 111–12
prisoners of war, 85–86, *86*, 222
publicity. *See* news and publicity
"Purple" code, *97*

radiation, 77, 201, *257*
Rayburn, Sam, 35
relocation centers, *263*, 263–64
Rhoades, Weldon, 168
Roosevelt, Anna, 36–37
Roosevelt, Eleanor, 36–37

Roosevelt, Franklin D., xii, *xii*, *262*, 263
  on atomic bombs, 88
  "Day of Infamy Speech" by, 265–67
  death of, 36–37
  Einstein and, xvi–xvii, 243–46
  on Manhattan Project, 88
  Pearl Harbor and, 262
  in Yalta conference, 15–19, *16*, *17*
Russell, Richard, 203–4
Russia. *See* Soviet Union; Stalin, Joseph

Sachs, Alexander, xiv, *xv*, xvi, 42
Sasebo Naval Station, 99
Shigemitsu, Mamoru, *232*, *233*
Shinto shrine, *202*
ships, *101*
  Augusta, USS, 157–61
  Bunker Hill, USS, *52*
  Indianapolis, USS, 71–73, 76
  Missouri, USS, 225–36, *226*, *236*
  Nashville, USS, 7, 10, 11
  Oneida, x
Sledge, Eugene, 46, 48
Solomon Islands, 44, 46
Soviet Union
  expansion of, 92
  Japan and, 18–19, 49, 116, 174–78
  in Manchuria conflict, 18–19, 49, 116,
    174–78
  Moscow, 49
  Patton on, 49
  START and, 273
  Yalta conference in, 15–19
Spaatz, Carl, *xiii*, xiv
  atomic bomb and, 102–3
  in Manila, Philippines, 102–6
Stalin, Joseph, xiv, *xv*
  goals of, 18
  Manchuria conflict and, 116, 174
  Okinawa and, 49
  in Potsdam summit, 61, *80*, *90*, 91–93
  Truman, H., and, 50, 61, 92–93

after World War II, 275
in Yalta conference, 15–19, *16*, *17*
START. *See* Strategic Arms Reduction Treaty
Stilwell, Joseph W., *30*
Stimson, Henry L., xii, *xiii*, 81, 210–11
on atomic bombs, 105
Stone, Harlan Fiske, 37, *38*
Strategic Air Forces, U.S., 102
Strategic Arms Reduction Treaty (START),
273
Strauss, Lewis L., 105
Supreme Council for Direction of War, 117,
206–8
Sutherland, Richard, *xiii*, xiv, 213
in Leyte, Visayan Islands, 10
Suzuki, Kantaro, xii, 116, 179, 206
Sweeney, Charles, xiv, *xv*, 120
Bockscar and, 188–99
in Hiroshima, 190–91
after World War II, 278

Target Committee, 42–43, 123
Taylor, Ralph, Jr., 120
theater group, 6
Tibbets, Paul W., xiv, *xv*, *115*
background on, 113, *115*
Bockscar and, 190, 191
Enola Gay and, *115*, *129*, 129–33,
136–40, 277–78
Little Boy bomb and, 113–15, 118–25,
119, 128–33, 136–42
in Tinian, Mariana Islands, 118–25,
128–33
after World War II, 277–78
time line, of World War II, 281–84
Tinian, Mariana Islands, 113–15, 113–25,
114, *120–21*, 128–33, 186–91
aerial view of, *120–21*
Tibbets in, 118–25, 128–33
Togo, Shigenori, 206
Tojo, Hideki, xii, *xiii*, 206–8, *207*, 260,
271–72

Tokyo Bay, 225–36, *242*
Tokyo bombings
B-29 bombers in, 24, 26–31, *27*
Doolittle raid on, 199
Hirohito during, 31, 32
LeMay in, *30*, 31, 34
M-69 firebombs in, 28–31, *29*, 34
on March 10,1945, 24–31
on March 18,1945, 32–34
Operation Meetinghouse and, 28–31
United States during, 24–34, 199
Toyama, Japan, 110
Toyoda, Soemu, 206
Trinitite, *77*, 77–78
Trinity
force measurements for, 126–27
success of, 69, *70*, 76–78
testing of, 58–69, *59*, *63*, *65*, *70*
Truman, Bess Wallace, *36*
Truman, Harry S., xii, *xiii*, *158*, *211*
on atomic bombs, 39–40, 81, 88, 91,
247–48
on *Augusta*, 157–61
in Berlin, 79–91, *89*
after Hiroshima bombing, 157–61
Japanese surrender and, 209–14, 218–20,
220, 225
MacArthur and, 165–66
after Nagasaki bombing, 203–4
opinions on, from subsequent presidents,
249–53
in Oval Office, 39–40
in Potsdam summit, 61, *80*, 87–93, *90*,
111–12
reflections of, 247–48
Stalin and, 50, 61, 92–93
taking oath of office, 35–40, *38*
Truman, Margaret, *36*, 227

Uehara, Shigetaro, 216
U.K. *See* United Kingdom
Ulithi Atoll, *101*

Umezu, Yoshijiro, 206, *232*
United Kingdom (U.K.), 273, 275
United States (U.S.). *See also* Hiroshima;
    Japan; Nagasaki
    Alamogordo Army Air Field, New
      Mexico, 78
    American Embassy, Tokyo, Japan, 237–40
    Americans, on atomic bomb, 169–71
    Doolittle raid by, 199
    Geneva Conventions and, 172–73
    in Guadalcanal, 44, 46
    Hague Conventions and, 172–73
    Hunter's Point, San Francisco, California,
      71–73
    Japanese Americans in, 263–64
    Jornada del Muerto Desert in, 42, 58–69,
      59, *60*, *70*, 76–78
    Leyte, Visayan Islands, and, 7–14, *9*
    Los Alamos, New Mexico, 2–6, 41–43
    Manhattan Project and, xii, 2–6, *3*,
      41–43, 58–69, *70*, 88
    Manila, Philippines, and, 20–23, 51–52,
      96–106, 165–68, 176–77
    during occupation of Japan, 241–42
    Okinawa Island and, 14, 44–49, *45–47*,
      57, 83, 99, 198–99
    Operation Coronet by, 100
    Operation Magic by, 98
    Operation Meetinghouse by, 28–31
    Operation Olympic by, *95*, 96–97,
      99–101, 105–6
    Pearl Harbor and, xvii, 73, 204, 260–62
    Peleliu, Philippines, and, 7, 8, 46–47, 99
    Potsdam summit and, 61, *80*, 87–93, *90*,
      111–12, 210–12, 218
    prisoners of war and, 85–86, *86*, *222*
    relocation centers in, *263*, 263–64
    Solomon Islands and, 44, 46
    START and, 273

    Strategic Air Forces, 102
    Target Committee, 42–43, 123
    Tinian, Mariana Islands, and, 113–25,
      114, *120–21*, 128–33, 186–91
    in Tokyo Bay, 225–36, *242*
    during Tokyo bombings, 24–34, 199
    on war crimes, 172–73, 224, 271–73, 274
    White House in, 39–40, 50, 203–4,
      209–14, 218–20
    in Yalta conference, 15–19, *16*, *17*
uranium, xvi, 28, 137
U.S. *See* United States

Wainwright, John, 234–35, *235*
war crimes, 172–73, 224, 271–73, 274
White House, 39–40, 50, 203–4, 209–14,
    218–20
World War II, xvi–xvii. *See also specific topics*
    announcing end of, 218–20
    Einstein after, 276–77
    Hirohito after, 241–42, 274–75
    MacArthur after, 274, 278–80
    Oppenheimer after, 275–76
    Stalin after, 275
    Sweeney after, 278
    Tibbets after, 277–78
    time line for, 281–84

Yalta conference
    Churchill in, 15–19, *16*, *17*
    purpose of, 16, 17
    Roosevelt, F., in, 15–19, *16*, *17*
    Stalin in, 15–19, *16*, *17*
Yamamoto, Isoroku, 260
Yamashita, Tomoyuki, xii, *xii*
    Leyte, Visayan Islands, and, 13
    in Manila, Philippines, 22
Yasukuni Shrine, 274–75
Yonai, Mitsumasa, 117, *117*, 206